Price $12.95

Encyclopedia of
# Victorian Colored Pattern Glass
# Book 4

# Custard Glass from A to Z

## by william heacock

**Featuring the collection of Mr. & Mrs. Dean L. Murray**

Photography by

**Dick Dietrich**

**Phoenix, Arizona**

Additional Photography by Richardson Printing Corp.

Published & Distributed by:

ANTIQUE PUBLICATIONS
Box 655
Marietta, Ohio 45750

Price $12.95
Accompanying price guide—$1.00

# DEDICATION

To Dean L. Murray

and his lovely wife Jane

Mr. Murray, author of two books on colored and art glass cruets, is an advanced collector of custard glass. The vast majority of the items shown in this book were from his collection, and this volume was published primarily due to his encouragement and faith in the project.

# TABLE OF CONTENTS

# HOW TO USE THIS BOOK

This volume is divided into the nine basic sections listed above in the table of contents. Each item is given a figure number for easier reference and for price guide listings. The patterns are classified according to their makers, except for Section 7, which includes several late additions to this book.

Care should be taken when advertising an item for sale with a Heacock reference number. The same numbers are used in volume after volume, so the volume number should always precede the figure number to avoid confusion with identical figure numbers from other books in this series.

Due to limited space for text below the color plates, frequently abbreviations are used to save space. An abbreviation key is included on page 10. An initial in parenthesis after a pattern name represents by whom the pattern received it's name. Often two or more names exist for a pattern. In most cases I used the pattern name assigned at the earliest date, except when a later name has proven to be more popular.

# ACKNOWLEDGEMENTS

This book was originally planned as a co-authorship - the sharing of efforts between two people devoted to this project, Dean L. Murray and myself. However, as production got under way we both became aware of the many problems faced in such a venture. Rather than continuing the joint partnership, I offered my services as a writer, researcher and production supervisor to Mr. Murray and "our" book, but I felt financial backing of the book should not be split between two good friends. There were just too many legal technicalities which needed defining.

I then received a phone call from Mr. Murray. Realizing that the project was just as important artistically to me as it was to him, he insisted that I take over the entire project myself. He gave me permission to photograph his extensive collection of custard glass, and helped me contact a local photographer. Dean and his lovely wife Jane provided priceless help during the photography sessions (2 very hot Arizona winter days), and made an unpleasant job almost delightful.

I am truly grateful to Dean and his wife for their patience during those days of production planning and photography. Dean has worked just as hard on this book as the author. He has travelled thousands and thousands of miles gathering together choice examples for this book; he sent out letters to dozens of custard collectors asking for help in documenting the "undocumented", and he kept me posted continually on his progress. Most of the "Late Additions" are included through his efforts. Thus, this book will remain as a testament of his dedication to the final product. I hope I have not failed him in my own efforts.

Certainly, there were others who were extremely helpful with this book. I can't go any further without thanking again Mr. Del L. Helman, his family and friends, for continuing to send me shards from the Northwood Glass Indiana, Pennsylvania plant site. Each box received resulted in new discoveries, and his trust in me makes me very humble.

A new name listed in these credits: J. Christopher Ramsey. Mr. Ramsey has been scourging the Library of Congress for any promising bits of information which might prove important to my work, and I am quite grateful for his efforts to date.

A special word of thanks to Mr. & Mrs. Jerry Volkmer for providing me with several rare and unusual examples for this book, and for continually keeping me posted on anything they find in colored glass which they feel deserves documentation.

And I don't want to forget my good friends the Heischman's, the Elliot's, the Goldsberry's, Loren Yeakley, Dick Marsh, Lenna Shaw, and Mr. and Mrs. Dale Ender for their contributions to this volume.

My usual big thank you to the staff of Richardson Printing Corporation, whose continued patience, advise and other efforts have helped me more than I can express here, and a special thanks to my secretary Pam Richardson who is helping take over some of the tremendous burden of producing these books.

My final thank you is to the primary photographer of this book, Dick Dietrich. He is a terribly conscientious individual, and I anxiously look forward to working again with this patient, pleasant and talented man. Others involved in photography were Dale Brown and Jack Hall.

# INTRODUCTION

A quick scan through the pages of this book will reveal to many of you readers the true beauty of the popular glass which is known today as "custard" glass. This book is the fourth in a series on colored pattern glass made between the years 1885 to 1910, with each volume devoted to a specific subject.

The colored glass field is so diversified that it may take a dozen volumes or more to cover it adequately. You will note I use the word "adequately", not "completely". I enjoy researching and documenting glass, but there are thousands of facts which will never be known, no matter how much I dig. Nor do I claim that all of the answers I turn up should be considered the complete and final results. The continued research undertaken by myself and others will undoubtedly turn up clues which can cast doubt on some of the data presented in this series. I am making no attempt to set myself up as the final authority in this field of pattern glass. Much of the data presented in this series has been documented previously by other historians. However, a considerable amount of new information has been turned up in the dozens of years since most of these early references were first written.

Thus we have the purpose of this series, to present updated information; to consolidate data from a dozen different sources, along with my own research findings, into one single source. I am not claiming to be any more knowledgeable than our early glass writers. This series would not have been possible without their works. However, as is undoubtedly the case with any researcher in any field, I am apparently setting myself up for criticism.

Just exactly what is glass research? It is digging for unpublished facts. It is studying dozens of collections of glass closely for important details which might prove essential to their documentation. It is visiting glass museums all over the country. It is writing and receiving hundreds of letters from collectors, dealers and other writers in this field. It is filled with many hopeful clues, and just as many "dead ends". It is essentially a fulltime occupation offering limited rewards, and a single critical letter can sometimes destroy the feeling of accomplishment built up by dozens of favorable letters. Perhaps this criticism is for the best, however. It makes me work that much harder for accuracy, for more complete answers to plaguing questions, for better and more exciting publications.

I am honored by the response this series has received to date, yet I am sadly aware of the drawbacks to it. As my research continues for each successive volume, new facts are turned up which prove data presented in earlier volumes to be incorrect. I have made a concerted effort to correct these known mistakes by listing them in successive volumes, but many readers of my books are limited in their interests to a specific subject (i.e., toothpick holder collectors only own Book 1). These readers are not aware that some of the data presented there has been proved wrong, and that dozens of rare colors can now be added to those already listed.

This unfortunate situation is indeed worthy of condemnation, if it were not for the fact I am making a distinct effort to correct these mistakes in later editions of the same volumes. This series is not quite two years old as yet, but Book 1 was recently revised and reprinted in a much more accurate second edition. However, it is sometimes maddening that in the process of answering a few questions, countless more sprout up as a result. I trust that my critics will try to be more patient with me in the future, and perhaps by the time we reach the fourth or fifth printing, we will finally get it right. Believe me, the accuracy of these books is as important to me as I am sure it is to my readers.

# CUSTARD GLASS

Custard glass derives it's name from the creamy yellow-white color in which most pieces can be found. The term was assigned many years ago by collectors who requested glass at antique shops, "Do you have any custard colored glass?" This was before any decent reference materials were available and glass lovers bought glass for it's color or design, not really caring who made it, just as long as it was old.

This lovely colored glass was introduced around 1895 in the United States and originally it was called "ivory" by most manufacturers. The color often varies from an opaque off-white (almost a milk glass), to a rich yellow-green opaque. The density of the glass also varies, from thick and solid to a light and transluscent quality.

Much has been written previously, concerning the high and low uranium salt content of certain patterns in custard glass, and I will not be repetitious here. However, the higher the uranium content, the more luminous yellow the glass appears. Most of Northwood's custard lacks a high uranium content, whereas the Heisey custard has a high content and luminescence.

Today, custard glass is highly collectible and pieces are disappearing from the market, driving prices up gradually. For some time only carnival glass sets were bringing prices comparable to or better than custard, but today opalescent glass sets are running a close third.

# CUSTARD GLASS PATTERN POPULARITY

A poll was taken in 1967 and again in 1973 of the members of the American Custard Glass Association as to which patterns in custard glass they thought were most popular. It should be noted that there was little published material on custard glass at the time of the earlier poll. It is also conclusive that the availability of these patterns may have had something to do with their popularity. My own personal favorite patterns are Beaded Circle and Victoria, primarily because of their unusually delicate hand decoration, but also because they are so terribly scarce.

| 1967 POLL | 1973 POLL |
|---|---|
| 1. Argonaut Shell | 1. Chrysanthemum Sprig |
| 2. Inverted Fan & Feather | 2. Argonaut Shell |
| 3. Chrysanthemum Sprig | 3. Inv. Fan & Feather |
| 4. Louis XV | 4. Louis XV |
| 5. Intaglio | 5. Ivorina Verde |
| 6. Geneva | 6. Intaglio |
| 7. Maple Leaf | 7. Northwood Grape |
| 8. Beaded Circle | 8. Diamond with Peg |
| 9. Ivorina Verde | 9. Maple Leaf |
| 10. Northwood Grape | 10. Georgia Gem |

I thought it might interest my readers to know, in correlation, which are the ten *rarest* patterns in custard glass according to my researcher's opinion. Oddly enough, the fact that these are so rare today in table settings is, in some cases, due to the fact that the patterns did not sell well when originally produced. Other factors, however, may have caused their limited production. Some are rare because their present owners appreciate their beauty so much, thus preventing the glass from appearing on the market. The listing below refers to table setting pieces—not souvenir glass!!! Piecing together some of the five rarest sets would be a near impossibility.

## TEN RAREST PATTERNS

| | |
|---|---|
| 1. Jefferson Optic | 6. Wild Bouquet |
| 2. Tiny Thumbprint | 7. Diamond Maple Leaf |
| 3. Cane Insert | 8. Everglades |
| 4. Beaded Circle | 9. Ribbed Drape |
| 5. Victoria | 10. Trailing Vine |

Other rare patterns, Delaware and Ribbed Thumbprint, are known only in incomplete sets in custard. Both are found in tumblers and creamers, which would imply a table and water set were made, but these sets have not been documented to date.

# A BRIEF HISTORY OF CUSTARD GLASS

A type of glass which has many of the qualities of custard was first made in England about 1880, primarily in small pressed glass table novelties (master salts, tiny handled baskets, salt dips, etc.). The British also used a formula on custard colored blown glass for an art glass line, usually with applied glass flowers or rigaree.

Bristol glass, made in England and other European countries, can also be found today in a rich custard color, frequently with delicate enamel decoration. Few examples of this European custard are shown in this book, as I chose to concentrate on American pattern glass.

There is some confusion as to just exactly when custard glass was first introduced in this country. Most sources credit Mr. Northwood with it's creation as early as 1887 (Millard states he may have first produced this glass while still at LaBelle Glass Company that year). Kamm presents a theory that Northwood financed his first factory at Martins Ferry, Ohio for his new line of custard glass. She used the exact words "it is surmised", with no source of information provided for this claim. Unfortunately, she made this supposition underneath her essay on Chrysanthemum Sprig, never actually stating that the pattern was made at that early date, but virtually *every* writer since has dated that pattern around 1888. Thus, we find that there is no documentable proof that custard glass was made before 1890, whereas virtually all the pattern shards shown on pages 17 and 18 can be documented after 1896.

If we stick to facts, Dithridge & Company announced many lovely patterns in 1894, most of which are found today in a rich custard color. However, since the ads don't list the colors made, and since these patterns were made for several years, we cannot be certain who was first to introduce custard glass in America. It should be noted that Northwood's "ivory" color does not have the same luminous qualities found in the Dithridge pieces. It really is unimportant who was first. However, Northwood **was** the first to produce this glass for complete table settings.

About two years after Northwood first introduced his version of custard glass, other companies, envying the success of this new formula, created their own versions of custard glass for the American market with varying degrees of success, none of which equalled Northwood's. The A.H. Heisey Glass Company entered the market around 1898 (see ad reprint, pg. 61) with their most complete line, Ivorina Verde, better known today as Winged Scroll. U.S. Glass experimented with their version, a definite "ivory" color, beginning in 1899, and Tarentum introduced their rich custard color in 1900. Eventually Jefferson, Fenton and Dugan (Diamond) Glass made their contributions to the custard glass market. See the listing on page 8 for other companies with known custard production.

The peak years of production were from 1896 to 1908. Other custard was made after that year on a much more limited basis, as carnival glass was beginning to find it's market in America and a virtual dominance of the next ten years.

After 1915 custard glass resigned from the "table

set" era and entered an "art deco" era. The Cambridge and McKee Glass Companies made the primary contributions at this time, but without a doubt there were others. My knowledge of this glass, however, is considerably limited, and I am including only a few examples of this late custard production in this volume so that collectors can familiarize themselves with it's look.

During World War II and shortly afterward, use of uranium salts in glass was not allowed. Recently, custard glass reappeared on the market by glass companies specializing in the "nostaligic". However, in a few cases there were blatant attempts to reproduce originals and create a demand for a perfect copy. Fortunately, they rarely succeeded in their task, as the new custard lacks the quality and the "feel" of the old. However the untrained eye and the beginning collector will have some difficulty in detecting age.

# GLASS COMPANIES WHICH PRODUCED CUSTARD TABLEWARE

| COMPANY & LOCATIONS | Primary Years of Custard Production | Type of Custard Made |
|---|---|---|
| DITHRIDGE & CO., Pittsburgh, Pa. (Owned & operated the Fort Pitt Glass Works) | 1894-1908 | A true custard-yellow-opaque glass, in seasoning vessels (salt shakers, syrups, etc.) and lamps. Almost no table sets. |
| THE NORTHWOOD COMPANY, Indiana, Pa. | 1896-1904 | America's primary production of tableware, novelties, lamps; no souvenirs. |
| A. H. HEISEY GLASS CO., Newark Ohio | 1897-1910 | Tableware, souvenirs |
| CONSOLIDATED LAMP & GLASS CO. Fostoria, Ohio & Coraopolis, Pa. | 1894-1904 | Limited seasoning vessels, more ivory in color. |
| UNITED STATES GLASS COMPANY (Merger of several factories) | 1899-1910 | An imitation custard—a true ivory in tableware, novelties. |
| TARENTUM GLASS COMPANY Tarentum, Pa. | 1900-1905 | A rich custard glass, in tableware, often beautifully decorated—some souvenirs. |
| H. NORTHWOOD & CO., Wheeling, W. Va. | 1902-1922 | Tableware, novelties, lamps |
| JEFFERSON GLASS COMPANY Steubenville, Ohio Williamstown, W. Va. | 1904-1915 | Tableware, novelties & souvenirs |
| DUGAN GLASS COMPANY DIAMOND GLASS-WARE COMPANY Indiana, Pennsylvania | 1904-1915 | Continued production of Northwood patterns, designed others of their own (no souvenirs—few novelties). |
| COUDERSPORT TILE & ORNAMENTAL GLASS COMPANY, Coudersport, Pa. | 1900-1904 | Limited tableware, seasoning items |
| FENTON GLASS COMPANY | 1907-1913 | Some tableware, mostly novelties |
| IMPERIAL GLASS COMPANY | 1908 | Limited—mostly novelties |
| CAMBRIDGE GLASS COMPANY | 1908-1920 | Two shades of custard in designs reminiscent of the Art Deco |
| McKEE GLASS COMPANY Jeanette, Pa. | circa 1915-1930 | Late custard ware (dinnerware, planters, lamp globes) |

# SUPPLY AND DEMAND

## *A Personal Look at an Inflationary Market*

With the rising popularity of colored glass of the Victorian era, I find that an educated buying public creates a healthy market. Since publication of Volume 2 of this series, I have watched in amazement as some asking prices surpassed my value guides by as much as 50%. And some pieces were even *selling* for these almost incredible prices.

This spiralling, inflationary trend has caused some resentment among a hand full of glass dealers, who claim they are no longer able to buy at a price where they can re-sell. Thus, they are forced to pay higher prices for stock and, with an acceptable business mark-up, the price tags frequently are embarrassing. Thus, dealers complain to me that my value guides are sometimes way too low. And collectors sneer that if they want anything worthwhile to add to their collection they are having to pay more than I say the things are worth.

It seems as though I am always defending myself these days, and it is not a pleasant position to be in. Perhaps I can explain my motives, and offer insight into these unfortunate results over which I have no control.

Contrary to what people think, *everybody* does not have my books and price guides. I wish they did. I wouldn't have to write another word as long as I lived if that were true. Only I know how many copies of my books are in distribution, and let me assure you that less than one-tenth of one percent of all the antique dealers in this country have my books. Naturally, many of the serious colored glass collectors have at least one of the volumes. But there are still thousands of "hobby" collectors out there who don't realize the value that education has in this field.

As for those rapidly increasing prices, I have a simple explanation. Before publication of Book 2, a cranberry opalescent blown pitcher rarely sold for $125. Now these pitchers (except for the Coinspot and the Swirl patterns) easily sell for $200-$300. The reason for this is not my price guide—the reason is collectors are now educated. Before Book 2, everyone was afraid of reproductions in blown glass (courtesy of Wright and Fenton), and with a source of information to give them some assurances that their money was not being wasted, the investors soon started competing for the few pieces which were still available. These few pieces disappeared quickly, and dealers learning of this demand tried to meet the new demand. The wealthier collectors paid more and more for good pieces, dealers heard about some of these prices and they began to pay more and ask more for rare pieces when they were lucky enough to find them. And if they got these new higher prices, then the trend would continue on indefinitely.

Usually, the point can be reached where the "bottom falls out". The less affluent collectors cannot afford the new prices, wealthier collectors decide to shop around for more realistic prices, and a so-called "hot" item, priced at $300, is quietly sold a few months later for a more realistic $200.

Opalescent glass, especially the blown variety, is going through this mushrooming price rise right now. I cannot say just exactly when it will level off. It may continue for some time, as there is apparently a hungry market hunting for better pieces of glass, and new investors are joining the ranks every day.

My biggest concern is that the rise in these opalescent prices is happening too fast. I simply cannot list values in my guides according to what *one* desperate collector paid for a butter dish to complete her set. The prices quoted are realistic, fair retail, and I do not recommend it's usage by dealers.

Remember, not all antiques are safe investments. Because of reproductions I have heard stories of life-time collections selling at auction for less than the owner actually had invested. This is rare, to be sure. But as long as reproductions continue to glut the market legally, the value of buyer education becomes priceless. And an educated buying public is responsible for an inflationary market—not this author or his price guides.

As stated before, if it weren't for the fact that these value guides help increase the small market potential my books have, I would eliminate the guides altogether. They are intended to be used as a guide only, and there are far more "slow movers" shown in this series than "fast sellers". Knowing which patterns and pieces are in demand is the secret of success in this field, and my price guides do not reveal that.

While I am on the subject of inflationary trends, I feel a word is warranted concerning the spiralling cost of printing these books. Tremendous expense is involved in producing a color publication, especially of the quality I am trying to maintain. With each publication, the costs continue to rise, and even with dozens of cost-cutting features (i.e., condensing essential data on as few pages as possible), I am still unable to reduce the costs of each book. The market just isn't big enough yet to print the vast number of copies necessary to decrease the per book price. Paper costs are way up, advertising is an expensive necessity, and labor (at least 35 people have a personal hand in printing these books) is on the rise all the time. The only way that I could decrease their cost would be for each and every book to be sold at retail. This I tried with Book 1, but it did not work, and in order to let these books reach their full market potential, it was necessary to distribute them to wholesalers specializing in this field. The books are sold at virtual cost to these distributors. Every conceivable effort has been made to keep the cost to the reader at a minimum, without sacrificing the quality of the books. I just hate to cut out the ad reprints, to ignore the importance of including late additions just prior to publication, and as for the expensive color photography—well, that would be the last thing I'd sacrifice. The only answer is in the number of pages, so if the print seems a bit small and the words a bit too few, perhaps now you can understand why.

# BIBLIOGRAPHY REFERENCES

| AUTHOR | REFERENCE | PUBLISHER |
|---|---|---|
| Gaddis, James H. | "Keys to Custard Glass Identification" | Early America Co. Pontiac, Ill. |
| Hartung, Marion T. | "Northwood Pattern Glass in Color" | Wallace-Homestead Des Moines, Iowa |
| Hartung, Marion T. | "Opalescent Pattern Glass" | Wallace-Homestead Des Moines, Iowa |
| Hartung, Marion T. | "Carnival Glass in Color" | Wallace-Homestead Des Moines, Iowa |
| Heacock, William | "Encyclopedia of Victorian Colored Pattern Glass," Volume I | Antique Publications Marietta, O. |
| Heacock, William | Same, Volume II | Antique Publications Marietta, O. |
| Heacock, William | Same, Volume III | Antique Publications Marietta, O. |
| Kamm, Minnie W. | Series of 8 Books on Pattern Glass | Kamm Publications Grosse Point, Mi. |
| Metz, Alice H. | "Early American Pattern Glass" | Author |
| Metz, Alice H. | "Much More Early American Pattern Glass" | Author |
| Millard, S.T. | "Opaque Glass" | Central Press Topeka, Ks. |
| Olson, O.J. | "Custard Glass Partyline" (Periodical of American Custard Glass Association) | A.C.G.A. Kansas City, Mo. |
| Peterson, Arthur | "Glass Salt Shakers—1,000 Patterns" | Wallace-Homestead Des Moines, Iowa |
| Peterson, Arthur | "Glass Patents & Patterns" | Celery City Printing Sanford, Fla. |
| Presnick, Rose | Series of 4 Books on Carnival Glass | Banner Printing Wadsworth, Ohio |

# ABBREVIATION KEY

A — Name by Author or variation by myself
K — Name by Kamm
OMN — Original Manufacturer's Name
P — Name by Peterson
G — Name by Gaddis
M — Name by Metz
Pr — Name by Presnick
H — Name by Hartung
PN — Popular Nomenclature

souv. — souvenir or souvenired

o.s. — original cruet stopper
n.o.s. — not original stopper
a.k.a.—also known as
Y.O.P.—year or years of production
repro—reproduction
opales.—opalescent
Fig.—figure number
pg.—page
decor.—decorated or decoration
jelly—jelly compote
pitcher—water pitcher, unless otherwise noted

# Custard Glass by
# Northwood & Associates

Including Patterns Made by:
The Northwood Co., Indiana, Pa.
H. Northwood & Co., Wheeling, W. Va.
Dugan Glass Co., Indiana, Pa.
Diamond Glass-Ware Co., Indiana, Pa.

Fig. A
**GENEVA**
(banana boat)

# HARRY NORTHWOOD —
# THE KING OF CUSTARD PRODUCTION

As is evidenced by the number of pages devoted here to his glass, Mr. Harry Northwood was the primary producer of custard glass in America. He appears to have introduced his version of this creamy opaque glass around 1896, and continued to produce it as late as 1920. He started with production of table ware at his Indiana, Pennsylvania factory and introduced additional patterns after he relocated to Wheeling, W. Va. in 1902.

Most of his patterns were made at the Pennsylvania factory, and it is not known whether he retained molds at the time he relocated. There are some indications that it is at least possible. An example is the goofus decoration found on opalescent pieces of **Wild Bouquet.** A theory presented in Book 1 was that since Northwood patented this decoration technique in 1904, that certainly these pieces must have been made at the Wheeling location. Again, it was a theory. Since pieces of glass in **Wild Bouquet** have been dug up at Indiana, Pa. in all colors, and since the pattern is quite rare today in all colors, I doubt very much that it was made in two locations. Again, we find the case where "rules are made to be broken". Just when I think all the clues point to an obvious answer, I turn around and find another answer which reverses previous assumptions.

I personally doubt that Mr. Northwood would have been allowed to take molds with him when he left the National Glass Company, with whom he merged his Pennsylvania factory in 1899. After 1902, when Northwood opened his final factory at Wheeling, all existing ads feature new patterns, new ideas, and not a single known pattern predating 1900 has been documented as having been made again at Wheeling. Again, I am dealing here with theory, but a sound one, and remember—there are bound to be exceptions to any report based on theory.

Whereas it is not known if Northwood made any of his early patterns at his new location, it can now be reported that some of Northwood's later patterns were indeed made at Indiana, Pa. A considerable number of shards have been unearthed in the "Northwood Grape," along with a big chunk from a purple "Peacock at the Fountain" water pitcher. Both patterns are frequently seen with the *N-in-a-Circle* trademark, definitely attributable to Wheeling, and the latter pattern was patented by Mr. Northwood himself on July 7, 1914. Inasmuch as this discovery definitely tells us that Northwood did indeed retain some ties with his former associates at Indiana, Pa., it doesn't tell us exactly what. Apparently Dugan (Diamond) Glass did some sub-contract work on popular Northwood patterns. "Grape" and "Peacock" were two of Northwood's most popular lines, and he probably couldn't keep up with the demand. He must have called on his uncle, Mr. Dugan, and with proof that the two firms were so closely bonded by their family heritage and artistic background, I have titled this chapter "Custard Glass by Northwood & Associates."

Since we now know that a simple shard in a pattern neither proves it to be Dugan glass, nor disproves it to be Northwood glass, I frequently will refer to patterns which are in the least bit questionable as Northwood-Dugan. Without confirmed dates of production, this is the only answer. Diamond Spearhead is most decidedly a Northwood-Dugan pattern, as it has an estimated production date and pattern & color characteristics which are typical of both companies.

Whereas Northwood either designed or introduced most of the patterns shown in this section, at least two should be entirely credited to Dugan. These are the "Fan" pattern and the "Diamond Maple Leaf" patterns. The others are appropriately dated in the text, and yet we cannot rule out the possibility that some of them may have had continued production after Mr. Northwood cut off his ties with National Glass. Thus, I trust that there will not be too much objection among collectors as to the merits of the glass made after Northwood's departure, since it was all made with consistent quality inherited from it's brilliant founding father.

## BLUE CHRYSANTHEMUM SPRIG

Here we have a lovely form of glass which for several years was purchased by discriminating collectors as "rare blue custard", driving prices up astronomically over a relatively short period of time. Some early rumor started a real rush for this opaque blue glass, as it is even sought and admired by art glass enthusiasts. This is strange since Kamm, in her 1943 publication, called the color by it's proper nomenclature.

The whole craze, however, should be kept in perspective. The glass is indeed scarce today, but this is undoubtedly due to the surge of early collectors who bought up all available pieces prior to the search of present day enthusiasts. The word "rare" is used much too frequently in this case. I have studied at least a dozen collections which contained numerous pieces of blue **Chrysanthemum Sprig,** and yet I can list a hundred patterns of which I have never seen a complete set of any kind. It is those sets which deserve the connotation "rare".

No special chemicals were used to make this color any different from other forms of blue opaque glass, and the pieces are decorated with nothing more than Northwood's usual high standard of craftmanship.

I realize that I may be making some enemies by these rather harsh statements. I am merely trying to point out how easy it is for collectors to be misguided by rumors. I can recall in my early days of collecting that I turned down a dozen pieces of Spanish Lace with reeded handles (at prices which now make me sick) because several people told me that it had been reproduced. This is why accurate reporting is so important in glass research, and why older publications should be updated.

Despite all of the above, blue **Chrysanthemum Sprig** is still worth a considerable amount of money because of that magic word "demand". It is still highly sought after, and continues to remain a very good investment.

# THE NORTHWOOD-DUGAN
# GLASS DIGGINGS

Perhaps one of the most important developments in glass research in the past 10 years has been the unearthing of thousands of glass shards from the plant site at Indiana, Pennsylvania. This is the location where Harry Northwood opened a factory in 1896 and merged with the big conglomerate National Glass Company in 1899. Northwood pulled out in 1902 (yet the plant continued to carry his name and trademark), and the factory was eventually bought out by its managers in 1904, to become the Dugan Glass Company.

These diggings were undertaken by father and son Harry A. and Del L. Helman, ably assisted by George McMillan. I duly credited these three with words of praise in Volume 3 of this series, but since publication of that book I have received several additional boxes of glass dug up in early 1976. A glass researcher's dream is to have such a glorious opportunity to re-open doors to the past which clarify answers to dozens of questions plaguing collectors for years. So much research is based on "theory" (sadly, including my own), it is wonderful to have some undeniable documentation to present to my readers.

However, as many answers as are provided by these diggings, almost as many questions have come to surface. But at least we will have a better understanding of the glass industry at a time when much has been clouded by guess-work on the part of our research pioneers.

## THE GLASS SHARDS—
## JUST WHO MADE WHAT?

Perhaps the most difficult aspect of sifting through and studying these pieces of glass is attempting to date them. Dating each pattern is absolutely essential, since it provides accuracy in determining whether the pattern was made by Northwood himself, by the company bearing his name under the auspices of the big glass merger, by Dugan Glass or by the Diamond Glass-Ware Company (merely a name change around 1913).

There are several methods of dating the glass. The easiest way is to find a dated advertisement featuring the pattern in some way. This is where early wholesale catalogues provide such a valuable source of documentation. Even Sears catalogues have been known to help. Other less used methods are documented dates of purchase, although this is sometimes risky, and when all else fails, an instinctive guess based on years of study of glass of this era.

I have been criticized, perhaps justly, for this final aspect of glass research. I realize that this criticism is meant to be constructive, but seldom is it possible to

hit a bulls-eye with every guess. I try to use the terminology "probably" or "possibly", and even better yet, when my continued research efforts turn up a mistake, I correct it in future edition plannings, or print retractions through my columns in various trade journals. I have also been accused of being quick to point out mistakes in earlier publications (do they not notice that my own books receive this same judgement?) This may seem unnecessary to some, especially in the case of those researchers no longer living. They unfortunately cannot benefit from this generation's mushrooming interest in early glass which has helped release new efforts at research. But it definitely serves a purpose. If I claim Northwood made a pattern and Kamm or Hartung say it's Jefferson, I must weigh my proof against theirs for readers to take special notice that there is controversy. If I just made a simple statement as to the pattern's origin, then collectors in years to come will have two separate attributions to weigh, with one impervious to the other. At least by my pointing out the earlier conclusions, readers are more aware of the value of continued, updated research. It is not an attempt to discredit the great glass researchers. My only complaint is that the present editors of their priceless classics are ignorant to the value of correcting dozens of flaws. It is with these publishers that I have a legitimate bone to pick.

Thus, despite the terrific advantage I have as recipient of these pieces of glass found at the Northwood-Dugan site, I am still faced with a dilemma by the necessary presentation of some theories which may remain controversial among glass enthusiasts until future documentation either proves me wrong or proves me right. I am very much aware that some readers will consider this nothing more than guess-work, but it is based on substantial experience in the field, and all theories will be presented as just that, theories. I will present the facts to the best of my ability, and trust that my readers will accept the resulting conclusions as theory, not fact.

Before closing, I would like to touch on one more controversial matter. There are some who claim that these shards prove almost nothing because cullet was often sold from factory to factory. Cullet is broken pieces of glass which are melted down to form new glass. I cannot and will not discount the importance of these shards, as not one single piece of glass was turned up among them that could be attributed to any company other than Northwood and Dugan. There was no glass by McKee, Westmoreland, U.S. Glass, Beaumont or New Martinsville, all companies in existence at the same time.

# THE NORTHWOOD SCRIPT SIGNATURE—
# A PERSONAL THEORY

Only two patterns made in custard glass are adorned with the unique trademark, the name Northwood spelled out in script letters. These are Chrysanthemum Sprig and Argonaut Shell. Some sources have dated this trademark as early as 1888, and thus, the patterns as well.

However, this is decidedly most inaccurate. First of all, trademarks were rarely used until the turn of the century. Secondly, if Northwood had used this trademark at such an early date, why do only two patterns carry this mark? Why not any succeeding patterns of which Mr. Northwood was proud?

Having dealt with that theory, I will attempt to present one of my own. It is my belief that the Northwood script signature trademark was first initiated about 1898-1899, just prior to the company's merger into the National Glass Company. Since the factory was soon afterward owned by a big conglomerate, naturally the trademark was no longer used. Mr. Northwood himself went to England to head National Glass operations there, but the factory he worked so hard to organize continued to produce glass with his distinctive touch.

A non-pattern glass novelty, the "Town Pump & Trough", also can be found with the script signature. This unique creamer & open sugar was made in opalescent glass. Again, not all pieces found are signed.

Apparently this novelty was designed prior to Northwood's merger with National Glass.

Also, the tray used on the Nestor pattern cruet set is the same one used on Chrysanthemum Sprig's (see Book 3, pg. 58), and it sometimes carries the script trademark. Undoubtedly, the expense of re-tooling the molds to remove the trademark was not undertaken. I have also heard reports of the same tray in opalescent glass, although this is unconfirmed at this time.

One must remember, that after Northwood pulled out of National Glass in 1901, the factory he founded in 1896 continued to be called The Northwood Company until 1904. That was when National Glass leased the factory to it's managers, Thomas E. Dugan (Northwood's uncle) and W. G. Minnemeyer. It was then that the name was changed to the Dugan Glass Company. So for two years (1902-03), two different factories carried Mr. Northwood's name, undoubtedly an unexpected tribute to one of the leading figures in glass production at the turn of the century.

After Northwood opened his Wheeling Factory, he introduced his new, more realistic trademark—the *N-in-a-Circle*—in 1905. The script signature was no longer ideally suited for a more streamlined and cost-conscious industry.

*(Note that the letters are backwards)*

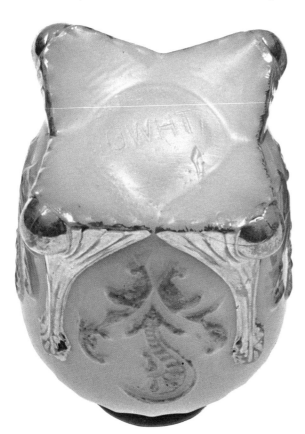
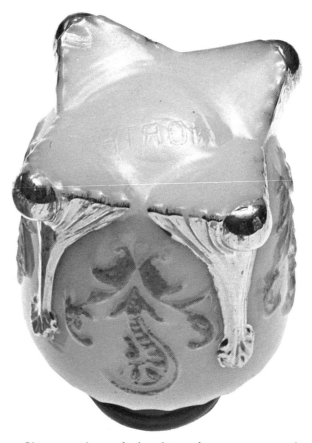

Close-up shot of the heretofore controversial Northwood "block letter" signature, found only on the base of the *Inverted Fan & Feather* salt and pepper.

14

# THE NORTHWOOD-DUGAN DIGGINGS—ADDITIONAL PATTERN REPORT

In addition to the pattern shards reported to you in Volume 3, the following should be added to that listing. I am making no attempt, however, to name which was Northwood's, which was Dugan's or which were a combination of both companies' efforts, as I am learning this is far too risky and that it gives birth to too much criticism.

INVERTED FAN & FEATHER—the custard glass pieces shown here, as well as the pink slag, and a very rare chunk from a green opaque piece. Also enough shards from those novelties in vaseline and blue were turned up to confirm now that Figure 612 (Book 2) is not a reproduction, and I apologize to my readers who were inconvenienced in any way by my adhering to rumors.

DOLPHIN PETTICOAT CANDLESTICKS—several pieces in white and blue.

SPANISH LACE—a finial from a white opales. butter lid, and almost an entire salt shaker in crnbry (same as Book 2, Fig. 322)

BUTTON PANEL—my apologies to Coudersport, but several pieces of this have been unearthed in all colors. Perhaps the molds were transferred after Coudersport closed in 1904 and Dugan Glass continued production.

TOWN PUMP—also have a handle in canary.

OPAL OPEN—several pieces in all colors.

QUILTED PHLOX—a real thrill to find a piece in white opaque, confirming my theory from Book 3.

PANELLED SPRIG—a big piece in white opaque, several in cranberry.

DOLPHIN COMPOTE—a base in canary, many more pieces in blue & crystal.

TWIG VASE and TINY TWIG—pieces in canary, crystal & carnival.

PRESSED COINSPOT—pieces of this novelty in carnival.

RAMBLER ROSE (Har Car 2,86)—marigold carnival.

CARNIVAL SWAN—many shards in this novelty: Presnick calls it a master salt.

BLOWN DRAPE—a large piece in green opalescent.

FEATHER & SCROLL—(Presnick 3, #62)—a piece in emerald green; pattern was also made in carnival colors; Hartung calls this "Quill".

And remember, there are hundreds of other pieces which I have not yet been able to identify. Dozens in carnival, scores in depression glass colors, a few opaque patterns I don't recognize, and many many more. I am studying these further for later reports in this series.

# PATTERN INDEX TO CUSTARD GLASS SHARDS

## SHARD A— *Chrysanthemum Sprig*

I start with this pattern simply because there were more custard and blue opaque pieces in it than in any other. Also, although there seems to be no proof, most sources claim that this was Northwood's first venture into custard glass production. See my notes concerning this theory on page 7.

Due to the vast number of shards found in **Chrysanthemum Sprig** (only a few are shown on pages 17 & 18), the pattern undoubtedly met with tremendous success when introduced. But just exactly when was it introduced? In 1888, as Kamm and Hartung allude, or after 1896, as I claim based on information provided by a box full of bits of glass?

To the best of my knowledge, there is not one single advertisement predating 1896 which mentions Northwood's "ivory" colored production. I cannot rule out the possibility that he may have experimented with custard production before this date, but I will say it is highly unlikely.

In Kamm 5, page 88, she states "the next year (1898) 'Klondike' came out," referring to the **Chrysanthemum Sprig** pattern. At first I thought this to be a mistake, since the known **Klondyke** (Note the spelling) pattern is better known today as **Fluted Scrolls** (see my Book 2, pg. 100). However, Kamm again makes a similar reference to the introduction of C. S. in her own Book 2, page 100. An explanation of this mystery is not possible, but the date seems to confirm my theories concerning this pattern's production date, location and the date of Northwood's script signature trademark.

Without much doubt, the extraordinary number of pieces unearthed at Indiana, Pa., lead me to believe that **Chrysanthemum Sprig** had its primary years of production at this factory, and that it was introduced there as well, and not at Martins Ferry, Ohio.

## SHARD B— *Argonaut Shell*

This pattern definitely made it's appearance at the Indiana, Pa. factory, although one source dates it earlier due to the script signature which was thought to date from Northwood's early production. Shards were found in **Argonaut Shell** in custard, opalescent colors & crystal.

The shards and their production date confirm Kamm's theory that the "Nautilus" pattern, advertised in 1900 by Northwood (with no illustration), is the one known today as **A.S.**

My own theory that the molds were transferred to Northwood's Wheeling factory appears now to be incorrect. That assumption was based on the fact that **A.S.** was made later in carnival glass novelties, and Dugan (Diamond) was not known to have produced irridescent glass, a supposition now known to be false.

## SHARD C— *Jackson*

Unfortunately, I endorsed the name Jackson for this pattern in my Volume 2 on opalescent glass. This other name was initiated by Brahmer in her book on custard glass, and I was mistaken in judging the public acceptance of the terminology. However, because of my book, the name for this varient of **Fluted Scrolls** (also known as **Fluted Scrolls with Flower Band**) seems now to be catching on, and I suppose it is best to have separate names for the two patterns. Other than the band of flowers, the only difference between the two patterns is the size of the cruets.

A good number of shards were found in these two patterns in opalescent colors, considerably fewer in custard. However, the shards confirm nothing more than a well-known fact that this pattern was introduced in the city of Indiana by Mr. Northwood in 1898 (original name: **Klondyke**). Production was undoubtedly continued for several years, perhaps even after Northwood's departure from the firm.

## SHARD D— *Intaglio*

Again, the shards found in this pattern merely confirm the previously confirmed production of **Intaglio** at this plant. The pattern

was advertised by the Northwood Company in 1898 in custard and emerald green. The opalescent production apparently followed some time later. Shards in all three types of glass are prevalent.

## SHARD E— *Louis XV*

Almost as many shards in this pattern have turned up as have in Chrysanthemum Sprig. These shards confirm known production of this pattern at Indiana, Pa. Louis XV was advertised beginning in September, 1898, in ivory and gold (custard). It was also produced in emerald green, but no shards have been found yet in this color.

## SHARD F— *Inverted Fan & Feather*

It's origins shrouded in mystery for many years, the unearthing of dozens of shards in this pattern has provided almost as many questions as it has answers. The exact date of introduction is not known, although reportedly the pattern was designed by Mr. Northwood himself in 1900. Shards of the pattern abound in custard glass and opalescent colors. Apparently the pattern was never made at Northwood's Wheeling location. Most researcher's theorized, including myself, that primary production of this pattern was at his Wheeling, West Virginia factory.

By far the most exciting and puzzling shard in this pattern is the piece from a punch cup in a unique green opaque satin. As a color experimentalist, Mr. Northwood has become something of a problem to a researcher trying to document his colored glass production.

## SHARD G— *Wild Bouquet*

I was wrong again. This pattern was not made at Northwood's Wheeling location, but at the Indiana, Pa. factory. Several shards have been found, in both custard and colored glass. Hartung reports the pattern was advertised in 1902, which could correspond with either Northwood factory (both carried his name). Production was limited, as the pattern is rare in all colors.

## SHARD H— *Maple Leaf, Northwood's*

A single shard in custard has been found in this pattern at Indiana, Pa. It is an "arm" off the spooner. However, two substantial pieces in carnival glass were also dug up.

Undoubtedly, Mr. Northwood had a strong hand in the design and creation of this beautiful naturalistic pattern. However, the existence of the carnival shards offers strong proof that the pattern was made also by the heirs at the Diamond Glass-Ware Company.

No definite date of production can be ascertained, and it is not known whether production of the pattern ever was undertaken at Wheeling. Hartung implies that the pattern is sometimes signed with the N-in-a-Circle trademark, but this is unsubstantiated by her text (Carnival Glass in Color).

Kamm named the pattern in her Book 5, attributing the pattern only by design and color characteristics, a method often used by myself—and one occasionally subject to criticism.

## SHARD I— *Fan*

A good number of pieces in this pattern have been found at the factory site, and I have taken it upon myself to remove the name Northwood from it's identification. In Book 2 of my series, I stated that if Dugan Glass could be credited with carnival glass production then I felt the pattern should be credited solely to Dugan. Indeed they did produce a vast amount of carnival glass. Hundreds and hundreds of shards attest to this long overlooked fact. Add to this the occasional piece of **Fan** found signed with the **D-in-a-Diamond** trademark of Dugan (later Diamond Glass-Ware), and the **facts** pretty much discredit the previous Northwood attributions showered upon this pattern. The name of the pattern is apparently a Hartung creation.

**CUSTARD SHARDS**
**Found at**
**Indiana, Pa.**

**CUSTARD SHARDS IN COLOR**—(A) Chrysanthemum Sprig, (B) Argonaut Shell, (C) Jackson, (D) Intaglio, (E) Louis XV, (F) Inverted Fan & Feather, (G) Wild Bouquet, (H) Northwood Maple Leaf, (I) Fan.

17

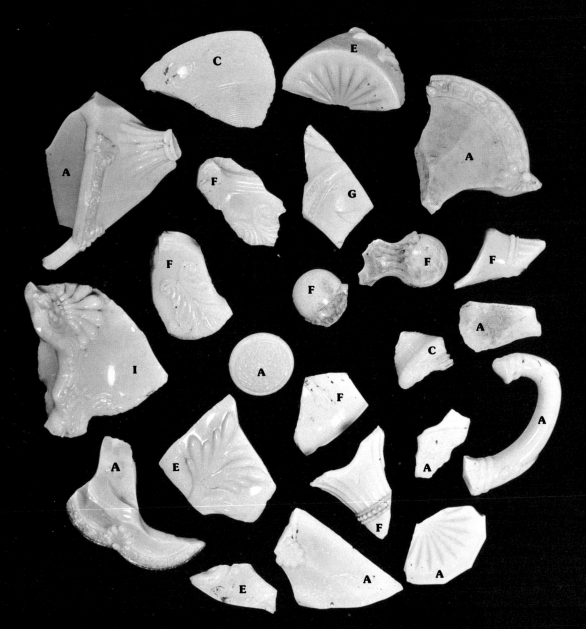

**CUSTARD SHARDS**
Found at
Indiana, Pa.

CUSTARD SHARDS IN COLOR—(A) Chrysanthemum Sprig, (B) Argonaut Shell, (C) Jackson, (D) Intaglio, (E) Louis XV, (F) Inverted Fan & Feather, (G) Wild Bouquet, (H) Northwood Maple Leaf, (I) Fan.

Inverted Fan & Feather (W)

PUNCH BOWL & CUPS
1
2

# Inverted Fan & Feather (W)

| 3 SALT | 4 JELLY | 3 PEPPER | 5 TUMBLER | 6 PITCHER | 5 TUMBLER |
| 7 BUTTER | 8 SUGAR | 9 SPOONER | 10 CREAMER |
| 11 TOOTHPICK | 12 CRUET (o.s) | 13 BERRY | 14 MASTER BERRY | 13 BERRY |

**INVERTED FAN & FEATHER** (Figures 1-14) Undoubtedly one of the most beautiful patterns created by Northwood in *any* color. It was designed by Mr. Northwood himself around 1900, and reportedly was featured at the Pan American Exposition at Buffalo, N.Y. in 1902. Shards on pages 17 & 18 appear to confirm my theory that this pattern was made at Northwood's Indiana, Pa., factory, and not at his Wheeling location, as most sources theorize. Shards have been found in all colors in this pattern, which seems to confirm the theory that production of I.F. & F. continued after Northwood's 1901 departure. The National Glass Company had a massive display at the Buffalo Exposition, and were especially proud of the pink slag in this pattern. All pieces known made are shown here, with the possible rare exception of a novelty dish of some kind in custard. Less than four punch bowls have been documented to date.

The salt shakers are rarely found signed Northwood in *block*

letters. The name is usually indistinguishable, as the letters are all backwards (a mold maker's error?) and often only a few letters are readable. See page 14 for a close-up of this mark.

I.F.&F. was also made around 1903 in opalescent glass, and the mold was later revived for limited production in carnival glass and opalescent novelties. I was incorrect in assuming that the rose bowls, ladies' spittoon's, and pulled vases were possible reproductions. I have sorted enough shards from these novelties to confirm that they are indeed products of the original maker; whether Northwood or Dugan—it should make no difference.

The shard found in green opaque (page 17) is both fascinating and frightening. I anxiously await seeing my first entire piece in this color. It is without a doubt experimental, and it makes me even more aware that when it comes to Mr. Northwood, I can never out-guess him.

# Northwood Grape

| | | | | |
|---|---|---|---|---|
| **15**<br>HATPIN<br>HOLDER | **16**<br>TUMBLER | **17**<br>PITCHER | **16**<br>TUMBLER | **18**<br>COLOGNE |
| **19**<br>PIN TRAY | **20**<br>SPOONER | **21**<br>BUTTER | **22**<br>SUGAR | **23**<br>CREAMER |
| **24**<br>BREAKFAST<br>SUGAR | **25**<br>BREAKFAST<br>CREAMER | **26**<br>BERRY SAUCE<br>(pedestalled) | **27**<br>MASTER BERRY | **28**<br>BERRY<br>SAUCE |

**NORTHWOOD GRAPE**—This generally accepted name is used generically to include both the "Grape & Cable" and "Grape & Thumbprint" patterns. They are virtually identical in design, except for the thumbprints found on occasional table pieces, and there is no duplication of pieces in both patterns. The pattern was made in custard beginning around 1906, receiving popular market response, and later underwent even greater production in carnival glass. More pieces are known in carnival than in custard. Except for the items shown on these three pages, Northwood Grape was also made in a high-standard covered compote, a high-standard open compote (ruffle-edged), an ice cream set, candlesticks, a liqueur set (with

# Northwood Grape

30
**PUNCH CUP**

29
**PUNCH BOWL**

30
**PUNCH CUP**

31
**FERNERY**

32
**HUMIDOR**

33
**CENTERPIECE BOWL**

34
**2-HANDLED NAPPY**

35
**8" PLATE**
(six-sided)

36
**8" PLATE**

tiny shot glasses & a handled decanter), a sweetmeat, a single-handled nappy and a tiny perfume bottle. The pattern is usually stained in nutmeg brown on a shiny background, but is much more exciting stained in pink or blue on a satiny background. The sauces to the berry set can be either flat or pedestaled. The novelties and bowls can vary in the extent to which they are crimped. Most pieces are found signed with the Northwood **N-in-a-Circle** trademark. Shards of this pattern (in carnival colors only) have turned up at the Indiana, Pa. factory site, confirming the theory that the Dugan Glass Company did sub-contract work for Northwood on his more popular patterns. Name by Kamm 7, pg. 42.

# *Northwood's Grape*

# *Grape Arbor*

| 37 | 38 | 39 | 40 | 39 |
| --- | --- | --- | --- | --- |
| **PUNCH CUP** (blue decor.) | **PUNCH BOWL** (blue decor.) | **TUMBLER** (pink stain) | **PITCHER** (pink stain) | **TUMBLER** (pink stain) |

**41 CRACKER JAR**

**42 ORANGE BOWL** (pink stain)

**43 HUMIDOR** (pink stain)

**44 ORANGE BOWL** (flat-top)

**45 DRESSER TRAY**

**46 BANANA BOAT**

**NORTHWOOD GRAPE** (Cont.)—Note the difference between the humidor and the cracker jar, and that the large orange bowl can be either flat or ruffle-edged. All of the above were also made in carnival colors.

**GRAPE ARBOR** (Figures 39-40)—How sad that so few pieces were made in this exceedingly lovely pattern. It is known in both custard and carnival glass, but was made only in the water set and assorted novelties (bowls, vases, etc.). In custard glass it is quite rare in the water set, found decorated in nutmeg, pink and blue. The water pitcher is much lighter than most custard pitchers, as it is mold blown with an applied blown handle. Attribution is apparently based on the distinctive Northwood design, and the definitive color staining. Name by **Presnick.**

# *Intaglio* (OMN)

**47 CRUET** (o.s.)

**48 TUMBLER**

**49 PITCHER**

**48 TUMBLER**

**50 BUTTER**

**51 SPOONER**

**52 BUTTER**

**53 SUGAR**

**54 CREAMER**

**55 SALT**

**55 PEPPER**

**56 MASTER BERRY**

**57 BERRY SAUCE**

**58 JELLY**

**INTAGLIO** (Figures 47-59)—This is the original name assigned by Northwood to this pattern, which he introduced in 1898, while at Indiana, Pa. It was also made in opalescent colors of blue & white (novelties in canary), and in emerald green with gold. All pieces made are shown here, except for a possible novelty piece formed out of the berry sauce (have seen this in opalescent). No toothpick was made in this pattern, much to collectors' chagrin. In custard, the pattern is most often found decorated in green and gold, but it was also made with blue and gold decoration. The large master berry bowl (fig. 59) can be found in two sizes, either 7½" or 9" in diameter, offering credence to the theory that the larger is actually an open compote. The sauce was made in one size only, and it seems ironic that the expense of making two master berries would be undertaken.

# *Intaglio* (OMN)

# *Everglades*

**59 LARGE FRUIT COMPOTE**

**60 TUMBLER**

**61 PITCHER**

**62 JELLY**

**63 SPOONER**

**64 BUTTER**

**65 SUGAR**

**66 CREAMER**

**67 SAUCE**

**68 MASTER BERRY**

**69 SALT** (not custard)

**70 CRUET** (o.s.)

**69 PEPPER**

**EVERGLADES**—When this author turned up documentation that this pattern was proven Northwood, several previous theories by other researchers were abandoned. Some dated it as early as 1899. However, the pattern was "introduced" in 1902 by H. Northwood & Company as the "Carnelian" line. It was only made during the 1902-03 season, in both custard and opalescent glass. This explains Everglades high rating in the rarity listing on page 7. The salt shakers shown here have often been referred to as "light" or "weak" custard, whereas they are actually the vaseline opalescent shakers.

The blue opalescent shakers have the same opaline qualities (see Book, Fig. 226). The actual custard shakers are decorated with the same green and gold seen on the larger pieces, and are not nearly as transluscent. The name was given to this pattern by Mr. Bob Batty, famed pattern glass enthusiast, whose collection was featured by Kamm in her last two books.

All pieces known made are shown here. The pattern was also made in opalescent colors, and a few experimental pieces were made in purple slag.

# *Chrysanthemum Sprig* (K)

| 70 | 71 | 72 | 73 | 74 |
|----|----|----|----|----|
| **CELERY VASE** | **TUMBLER** | **PITCHER** | **CRUET SET** | **TOOTHPICK** |

| 75 | 76 | 77 | 78 |
|----|----|----|----|
| **SPOONER** | **BUTTER** | **SUGAR** | **CREAMER** |

| 79 | 80 | 81 | 82 |
|----|----|----|----|
| **CRUET** (blue opaque) | **JELLY** | **MASTER BERRY** | **SAUCE** |

**CHRYSANTHEMUM SPRIG** — Attribution of this pattern is simple; most pieces found are trademarked with the Northwood script signature. Dating it has been much more difficult, but this author dates the pattern from circa 1899 to 1904 (see notes on pg. 14).

This pattern is the one which was made in the expensive blue opaque, so highly regarded by some glass buffs that it is almost looked upon as art glass (see notes on pg. 12).

The custard is usually found decorated in sets as shown above. However pieces are also found less attractively decorated with goofus-type gold on the greek key border, and the flowers painted purple and red. This is an unfired decoration, not as pleasing to the eye of today's collectors. It is easily worn off, and many undecorated pieces of C.S. found today originally had this decoration on them. Some pieces have been seen entirely decorated in goofus, definitely most unappealing.

Care should be taken to avoid reproduction stoppers which have been released to match both stoppers shown on this page. The custard stopper does not match the true Northwood color and the blue stopper is made out of plastic, but is a very good match in color. The toothpick has been reproduced in all colors, but is easily distinguishable from the old toothpick shown here.

**83**
**JELLY**
(variant)

**84**
**JELLY**

**85**
**PITCHER**

**86**
**TUMBLER**

**87**
**CRUET**
(o.s.)

**88**
**SPOONER**

**89**
**BUTTER**

**90**
**SUGAR**

**91**
**CREAMER**

**92**
**SALT**

**93**
**PEPPER**

**94**
**TOOTHPICK**

**95**
**MASTER BERRY**

**96**
**SAUCE**

**ARGONAUT SHELL**—Kamm named this pattern **Argonaut** in the 1940's, but the two word name here seems to have caught on among glass collectors, perhaps due to it's endorsement by Millard, Presnick and Gaddis. All pieces known are shown here, except for a possible free-form novelty. The pattern is also found in opalescent colors and carnival novelties. The jelly compote can be found with or without the tiny sprig of seaweed. Shards of this pattern are prevalent at the Indiana, Pa. factory site, in both custard and opalescent. The pattern is usually graced with the Northwood script signature, and the speculated 1900 production date (Kamm reports a line called "Nautilus" was introduced that year) relatively confirms my theory about the date of this trademark. See notes concerning this on page 14. The stopper to the cruet is most intriguing, and I must admit I have never seen one like it which could be used in the opalescent cruet. The stopper to the custard cruet has been reproduced in a rubbery plastic.

# Northwood Maple Leaf (K)

**97 CRUET (o.s.)**

**98 JELLY**

**99 TUMBLER**

**100 PITCHER**

**101 TUMBLER**

**102 SPOONER**

**103 TOOTHPICK**

**104 BUTTER**

**105 SUGAR**

**106 CREAMER**

**107 SAUCE**

**108 MASTER BERRY**

**107 SAUCE**

**109 SALT**

**110 PEPPER**

**NORTHWOOD MAPLE LEAF**—All pieces known made in this lovely naturalistic pattern are shown here, including for the first time the very rare unlisted cruet with original stopper. This is the only one documented to date. A half dozen jelly compotes are known, and virtually all other pieces shown are at the least scarce today. Shards of this pattern have been unearthed at Indiana, Pa., which proves only that this pattern underwent some production there. Many sources attribute this to Northwood's Wheeling location. The pattern was also made in carnival colors as late as 1913.

Care should be taken not to confuse the sauce dish for a jelly compote. There is considerable difference in height and even more difference in value.

The pattern should be referred to as **Northwood Maple Leaf,** as there is another pattern made at the same factory known as **Diamond Maple Leaf** (see page 34, Fig. 187-190).

28

# Wild Bouquet (M)

| 111 | 112 | 113 | 112 | 114 |
| CRUET (o.s.) | TUMBLER | PITCHER | TUMBLER | SUGAR (with finial) |

| 115 | 116 | 117 | 118 |
| SPOONER | BUTTER (with arch) | CREAMER | SUGAR (with arch) |

| 119 | 120 | 121 | 120 | 122 |
| SALT | SAUCE | MASTER BERRY | SAUCE | TOOTHPICK |

**WILD BOUQUET**—This pattern was named by Metz, but Dr. Gaddis, thinking the name inappropriate, introduced a second name, **Iris.** Either name is accepted today—however, Iris is used primarily by custard collectors. Except for the jelly compote and the covered butter with standard finial, all pieces known made are shown here. The pattern is one of my personal favorites. It is quite rare today, perhaps because so many others appreciate it's beauty. Undoubtedly production was limited, however, since very few shards were turned up at the Indiana, Pa. diggings.

**Wild Bouquet** was also made in opalescent colors of white, blue and green, and has been reported, but not documented, in canary opalescent. The pattern is entirely different in shape and design

from any other Northwood line, and I am certain that he had a personal hand in it's design, even though the only known advertisement of this pattern dates it from 1902, that transitional date when two factories carried his name. I personally believe the custard was introduced around 1900 and the opalescent came later. See further notes concerning this pattern on page 12.

Pieces of **Wild Bouquet** have been studied in an unusual "grey" custard color, without decoration. It has a blue caste to its color, leading some collectors into thinking it is the color of blue **Chrysanthemum Sprig.** I believe it is nothing more than an off-color batch of custard. However, these pieces are extremely rare.

*Peacock & Urn* (H)

*Louis XV* (OMN)

| 123 | 124 | 125 | 126 | 125 |
|-----|-----|-----|-----|-----|
| MASTER ICE CREAM | INDIV. ICE CREAM | TUMBLER | PITCHER | TUMBLER |

| 127 | 128 | 129 | 130 |
|-----|-----|-----|-----|
| SPOONER | BUTTER | SUGAR | CREAMER |

| 131 | 132 | 133 | 134 | 135 |
|-----|-----|-----|-----|-----|
| SAUCE | MASTER BERRY | SALT | PEPPER | CRUET (o.s.) |

**PEACOCK AND URN** (Figures 123-124)—Without a doubt, this pattern was made at Northwood's Wheeling factory as it is usually signed with his **N-in-a-Circle** trademark. The pattern is often confused with "Peacock at the Fountain", of which only a few experimental tumblers are known made in custard. The pieces shown here are from an ice cream set, made by flattening the large berry bowl and small sauce, in which this pattern can also be found. A novelty, ruffle-edged, bowl may also have been made. It is stained with the distinctive Northwood nutmeg decoration.

**LOUIS XV** (Figures 125-135)—This is the original name for this pattern, which was produced beginning in 1898 at Northwood's Indiana, Pa. plant site. Shards found at that location confirm this date. All pieces known made are shown here. The pattern was also made in emerald green with gold, and strangely enough is one of the few patterns in custard not made in any way in opalescent. Occasionally this pattern is referred to as Winged Scroll, but this name should once and for all be eliminated. The pattern is graced with those distinctive Northwood-type feet.

# Northwood Beaded Circle (PN)

**(Figures 136-144)**

| 136 | 137 | 138 | 139 | 140 |
|---|---|---|---|---|
| **SPOONER** | **BUTTER** | **SUGAR** | **CREAMER** | **PITCHER** |

| 141 | 142 | 143 | 144 | 145 | 146 | 147 | 148 |
|---|---|---|---|---|---|---|---|
| **SALT** | **CRUET** (o.s.) | **PEPPER** | **MASTER BERRY** | **SALT** | **CRUET** | **PEPPER** | **MASTER BERRY** |

# Jackson

**(Figures 145-152)**

| 149 | 150 | 149 | 151 | 152 |
|---|---|---|---|---|
| **TUMBLER** | **PITCHER** | **TUMBLER** | **SUGAR** | **CREAMER** |

**BEADED CIRCLE** — The name for this pattern appears to be a popular nomenclature, but since there are other similarly named patterns, the Northwood name should precede it for proper identification. The pattern is not listed in any of our pioneer glass publications, which seems strange until one realizes how terribly rare this pattern is. I have only seen a few individual pieces for sale, never a set of any kind. It has a distinctive and delicate enamel decoration, with touches of gold on the beading.

Attribution of this pattern has been nothing more than public acceptance of it's origins to date. However the Oglebay Institute Museum has pieces of this pattern on display, attributed to Northwood, which were probably a portion of a collection of glass donated by Northwood's daughter, Mrs. Mabel Northwood Robb, to the Oglebay Institute. One source dates this pattern around 1895, but I am almost certain the pattern was made at Wheeling for two reasons. First, not one single shard of this pattern was dug up at Indiana, Pa. Second, the design of the pattern is so similar to other Northwood patterns, it leads me to believe that it was a compilation of ideas which lead to its creation. I date the pattern circa 1903-1904.

See also Figures 438 and 440 for pieces of Beaded Circle not shown here. Except for the berry sauce, all pieces known made are shown in this book. No toothpick or celery vase was made.

**JACKSON** — Named by Brahmer in her early custard glass publication, this pattern is also known as **Fluted Scrolls with Flower Band.** See notes on page 16 for further data concerning the name. Not shown in this pattern are the covered butter, spooner (straight-sided, slightly smaller in diameter than the sugar base), berry sauce and a novelty card tray, the latter usually found undecorated. The goofus decoration shown here is highly susceptible to wear, and the pattern is often found without decoration. The similar **Fluted Scrolls** pattern has no flower band on the design, and I feel they should be considered two distinct patterns since the cruets in both patterns are different in size and shape. Many shards of this pattern were unearthed at Indiana, Pa., and it dates from 1898 to 1904.

*Geneva*

| 153 JELLY | 154 TUMBLER | 155 PITCHER | 154 TUMBLER | 156 CRUET (o.s.) | 157 SYRUP |

| 158 SPOONER | 159 TOOTHPICK | 160 BUTTER | 161 SUGAR | 162 CREAMER |

| 163 MASTER BERRY (oval) | 164 SAUCE (oval) | 165 SALT | 166 SAUCE (round) | 167 MASTER BERRY (round) |

**GEVEVA**—Kamm states unequivocally that this pattern was by the Northwood Glass Co., but offers no proof of this claim. She reprints a page from an old Wards catalogue which dates this pattern as early as 1900, leading one to surmise that production took place at the only existing Northwood factory at that time, in Indiana, Pa. However, no shards in this pattern has been turned up in the recent diggings. This is inconclusive, I realize, but thought-provoking. It is also interesting that there was not one shard in chocolate glass, and **Geneva** underwent considerable production in this color. I strongly feel that this pattern was made at Wheeling, but with no proof, and only the 1900-01 Wards catalogue as a verification of the production date, the only possibility left is that Geneva had to be made at Indiana, Pa.

All pieces known made are shown in this book (see banana boat on page 11). The custard color is much paler than other Northwood custard, and is sometimes found without decoration. The pattern can be found decorated as shown above, in a lovely rust color (Figure 444) or in a fire-on green with gold decoration. The last two are quite hard to find. The berry set can be either round in shape or oval. Besides the rare chocolate pieces in **Geneva**, a rich emerald green with gold crystal was also made.

# Grape & Gothic Arches (Pr)

| 168 FAVOR VASE | 169 GOBLET | 170 TUMBLER | 171 PITCHER | 170 TUMBLER |
|---|---|---|---|---|

| 172 SPOONER | 173 BUTTER | 174 SUGAR | 175 CREAMER |
|---|---|---|---|

# Double Loop (Pr)

| 176 BREAKFAST SUGAR (open) | 177 BREAKFAST CREAMER | 178 SAUCE | 179 MASTER BERRY |
|---|---|---|---|

**GRAPE & GOTHIC ARCHES**—This rather simply designed pattern dates after 1905 and was made by Northwood at his Wheeling location. The custard color is a creamy white, sometimes stained with nutmeg brown, and sometimes simply trimmed in gold. Some pieces have been found iridised with a pearl-like finish, causing word to spread that it was some form of rare "custard carnival". This is a pattern where the rarest piece in the set is the one which is usually the most common in other sets—the small berry bowl. Mr. Murray spent many years in a diligent search for a sauce, and the one shown here was the fruit of his effort. All pieces known made, are shown here. The favor vase is a novelty formed from the goblet mold.

**DOUBLE LOOP**—This rare pattern has been seen by this author only in the breakfast-size creamer and open sugar pictured above. Presnick named this pattern, reporting it's existence in carnival glass, and mistakenly calls Figure 176 a chalice. I have seen the creamer in a deep cobalt blue (not carnival) with gold, and with the **N-in-a-Circle** trademark as proof of it's origin. As other pieces in this intriguing pattern are seen by me or reported to me, I will document them in a later volume of this series.

| 180 | 181 | 182 | 183 | 182 |
| MASTER BERRY | SAUCE | TUMBLER | PITCHER | TUMBLER |

## Fan (H)

| 184 | 185 | 186 |
| SUGAR | CREAMER | SPOONER |

## Diamond Maple Leaf (PN)

| 187 | 188 | 189 | 190 |
| SPOONER | BUTTER | SUGAR | CREAMER |
| (gold decor.) | (gold decor.) | (silver decor.) | (silver decor.) |

**FAN**—Except for the covered butter and possibly a novelty dish, all known pieces of this pattern are shown in this book. No toothpick, salt shaker or cruet have been reported to date. (See Figure 416-417 for the rare flattened ice cream set in this pattern, formed from the berry bowls.)

Many sources attribute this to Northwood, based on questionable evidence. I expressed my skepticism of this theory in Book 2 of this series, and I am now convinced that this pattern was indeed produced entirely by Dugan (Diamond), primarily because of the occasional piece of this pattern found with the **D-in-a-Diamond** trademark registered by the Diamond Glass-Ware Company in 1913. **Fan** was also made in opalescent colors (limited) custard carnival glass.

**DIAMOND MAPLE LEAF**—This rather striking pattern is entirely distinctive of the mold designers at Dugan Glass, well after North-

wood's departure from the firm. Two of the pieces shown here are signed with the **D-in-a-Diamond**. The handles and the finials are reminiscent of previous Northwood production, but the color of the glass and the extreme "business" of the pattern are Dugan's own. The pattern is found decorated richly with gold or silver. The silver decoration is not exactly an overlay. It is more like a brushstroke decoration. I am presently researching other Dugan patterns which are similarly decorated.

The Diamond name should always precede the pattern's name to differentiate from the Northwood version. The pattern was also made in emerald green, a rich cobalt blue, and a few novelties were made in opalescent glass. Only the table set, berry set, and a two-handled novelty dish, formed from the spooner mold, have been documented to date.

# Custard Novelties

| 191 THREE FRUITS | 192 GOOD LUCK | 193 DRAPERY | 194 POINSETTIA LATTICE | 195 SINGING BIRDS |

| 196 DANDELION | 197 BUSHEL BASKET | 198 FINECUT & ROSES | 199 BEADED CABLE | 200 GRAPE ARBOR | 201 SPOOL |

| 202 BEES ON A BASKET | 203 THREE FRUITS | 204 THREE FRUITS | 205 POPPY | 206 FLUTE |

**CUSTARD NOVELTIES**—most of the pieces shown here are proven Northwood, with only Figures 201 & 202 being questionable. These two pieces are also the only ones shown that can not be found in carnival glass. Since these are novelties, variations in shape frequently occur (i.e., Figures 191 & 204 are from the same mold). The nutmeg staining on most pieces is a distinctive "trademark" of Mr. Northwood's after his move to Wheeling, W. Va.

FIGURE 193—This is formed from a spooner mold; Circa 1906.

FIGURE 194—The distinctive blue shading is typically Northwood, confirming my attribution from Book 2; circa 1907.

FIGURE 195—This looks like a sauce dish to a berry set, but no large bowl has been reported to date, so it is more likely a small nappy; circa 1908.

FIGURE 197—Reproduced in several colors, some with the Northwood trademark still intact; circa 1910.

FIGURE 201—This may be a "Jefferson Spool" (see Book 2), but the color is not as rich as theirs usually is. This piece is either a spooner or open sugar, and a creamer was probably also made. No other pieces documented.

FIGURE 202—Attribution of this novelty toothpick is based on color clues. I have one in purple slag which has the same mosaic qualities of other Northwood slag. This can be found with or without a handle.

FIGURE 205—Also found without the ruffled edge; circa 1908.

# *Panelled Poppies*

207
**PANELLED POPPIES**

**PANELLED POPPIES**—I found this exciting hunk of custard glass at an antique show near where it was originally made. It is without a doubt Northwood glass, with a most unusual combination of nutmeg stain on a satin custard background. The glass is very heavy and thick, and susceptible to age crazing. Designed strictly for electrical lighting, this piece, which was made in Wheeling, I date around 1918. I received a letter, some time back, from a reader who had talked with a local old-timer. It seems this gentleman was a travelling salesman for Northwood just prior to the factory's closing. He said that the majority of the items he sold were lamps and lamp shades.

Originally this domed lamp shade may have had three similar matching shades which hung down from the main one, forming a chandelier of sorts. Mr. Murray is now the lucky owner of this lamp, and the photograph on page 3 shows the lamp as it is displayed in Mr. Murray's home.

# Custard Glass by
# A. H. Heisey Glass Company

Newark, Ohio

207-A
**PURITAN**
(rare compote)

207-D
**WINGED SCROLL**
(rare bulbous salt)

207-B
**WINGED SCROLL**
(decorated ring tree)

207-C
**BEADED PANEL & SUNBURST**
(rare punch cup)

# Winged Scroll

| 208 PITCHER (bulbous) | 209 TUMBLER | 210 PITCHER (tankard) | 211 VASE | 212 VASE | 213 VASE |

| 214 TOOTHPICK | 215 SPOONER | 216 BUTTER | 217 SUGAR | 218 CREAMER |

| 219 HUMIDOR (lid missing) | 220 CIGARETTE HOLDER | 221 MATCH HOLDER | 222 CELERY | 223 SALT | 224 SYRUP | 225 PEPPER |

**WINGED SCROLL**—Without a doubt, more different pieces were made in the pattern shown here than in any other custard glass pattern. As many as 50 different shapes are known, with only 36 of these shown in this book. Needless to say, many of the shapes listed in Heisey's catalogue were only free-form variations from the same mold. Yet it still boggles the mind to imagine a complete collection of this pattern.

A rare color advertisement of this pattern is reprinted on page 61 of this book. When first introduced about 1900, it was called **Ivorina Verde,** a reference to the "yellow-green ivory" color in which it was made. However, the pattern was also made in emerald green and in crystal, and thus the name would not apply here. This perhaps explains collectors' acceptance of the popular nomenclature "Winged Scroll". This was Heisey's #1280 pattern.

Certain pieces of the pattern are rare, including the cake stand, celery vase, covered humidor, high-standard compote and the bulbous salt shaker shown on page 60. Many other items are quite scarce, but the five items listed here can definitely be considered rare.

Pieces of the pattern have not been found signed with the Heisey trademark. Decoration of the glass varies, from brightly fired-gold to an unfired "goofus" type gold; from lovely delicate enamel decoration to no decoration at all; from green-stained "scrolls" to a rusty red stained scroll. A few rare pieces of the pattern have been found in vaseline and in milk glass.

See next page for listing of items made in this pattern. The pattern has been reproduced in a charming little miniature butter dish—however, not in custard glass as yet.

**226**
**HIGH STANDARD COMPOTE**

**227**
**CRUET**

**228**
**TRINKET BOX**

**224**
**COLOGNE**

**230**
**CAKE STAND**

*Winged Scroll*

**231**
**BON-BON**

**232**
**NAPPY**

**233**
**OLIVE DISH**

**234**
**PICKLE DISH**

**235**
**CUP & SAUCER**

**236**
**SAUCE**

**237**
**BERRY BOWL**

**238**
**MASTER BERRY**

**239**
**SAUCE**

**WINGED SCROLL**—Listing of pieces made: Table set, water set (bulbous or tankard pitcher), berry bowls and sauces in eight different sizes and shapes, a cake stand, 3 different high-standard compotes (flared out or up), celery vase, cruet (pressed or cut stopper), salt and pepper, syrup, toothpick, custard cup, puff box and trinket box, ring holder, hair receiver, 4" and 5" pin trays, cologne bottle, humidor, a cigar, cigarette and match holder, an ash receiver, an 8" or 10" tray, a 9" salver tray, a large tray on which most collectors display the dresser set, a 5", 6" and 7½" card receiver, blown vases in all sizes, a 5" and 6" plate (often used as a saucer for the cup), a 5" and 6" olive dish, a 5" and 6" pickle dish, a 5" and 6" Bon-Bon dish, a 5" and 6" ice cream nappy, and a 5" and 6" tri-cornered nappy. Add to this the very rare bulbous salt shaker, and the list is pretty much complete.

# Ring Band
(P)

| 240 | 241 | 242 | 243 | 244 | 245 |
|---|---|---|---|---|---|
| CELERY VASE | TOOTHPICK | TUMBLER (variant) | TUMBLER | PITCHER | TUMBLER |

| 246 | 247 | 248 | 249 | 250 | 251 |
|---|---|---|---|---|---|
| SALT | PEPPER | SPOONER | BUTTER | SUGAR | CREAMER |

| 252 | 253 | 254 | 255 | 256 |
|---|---|---|---|---|
| SYRUP | JELLY | CRUET SET TRAY | CUSTARD | CRUET (n.o.s.) |

**RING BAND**—This early Heisey pattern, oddly enough, never appeared in any of the pioneer glass publications, and in fact was named by Dr. Peterson in his book on salt shakers. The pattern was made only in custard, sometimes rich in color, sometimes quite pale, almost the color of milk glass. It was decorated in many different styles, but the most popular seems to have been the gold bands shown on Figure 244. Other forms of decoration are shown here, also. The toothpick, salt shakers and custard cup were frequently used for the souvenir market, as occasionally were the syrup and tumbler. The tumbler was made from two different molds, with the one shown as Fig. 242 designed to accomodate the enamel decoration. A rare ice cream set in this pattern is shown on the next page. The pattern dates from around 1901 and is occasionally found signed with the Heisey trademark.

# CUSTARD GLASS BY A. H. HEISEY

**257    258**
**CUT BLOCK**
indiv. sugar    indiv. creamer

**259**
master
ice cream
**RING BAND**

**260**
indiv.
ice cream

**261**
**WINGED SCROLL**
dresser tray

**262**
**PUNTY BAND**
souv. creamer

**263**
**PINEAPPLE & FAN**
souvenir pitcher

**264**
**BEADED PANEL & SUNBURST**
2-piece punch bowl

**265**
**PUNCH CUP**
(signed)

**266    267**
**BEAD SWAG**
goblet    wine

**MISCELLANEOUS HEISEY**—Occasional pieces of souvenir ware are found in patterns which received only minimal production in custard. These patterns include **Cut Block, Punty Band, Pineapple & Fan, Bead Swag,** and **Panelled Cane** (Fig. 422). Any unsouvenired piece of this pattern would be rare, so be careful to avoid pieces with the souveniring faded, scratched off or even professionally polished off.

CUT BLOCK (Fig. 257-258) The tiny individual creamer and open sugar are most often seen in this pattern as custard ware. A toothpick would be very rare.

RING BAND—see notes on previous page concerning this ice cream set.

WINGED SCROLL—this is the tray on which most collectors display the dresser set.

PUNTY BAND—also made in a souvenir open sugar and toothpick; others scarce

PINEAPPLE & FAN—this is the only piece reported in custard to date; common

PLAIN PUNCH CUP—all of the cups shown with the punch bowl are signed with the Heisey trademark. The cup can also be found souvenired. This cup and the Figure 398 cup have slightly different handles.

BEADED PANEL & SUNBURST—Very few of these punch bowls (2-pieces) are known to exist today. They are often subject to crazing, are extremely heavy, and have the richest custard color imaginable. This is a real museum piece! The cup made to match this bowl is equally rare. (See also Book I.)

BEAD SWAG—Found in goblets and wines, the former frequently souvenired, the latter less often. Any other piece in custard would be rare.

269

270

271

268

## Winged Scroll Smoke Set

**(Humidor, cigar holder & cigarette holder on tray)**

The match holder and ash receiver (shown elsewhere in this book) were also made to go with this set, but do not fit on the tray shown here. A larger tray was made, perhaps to accomodate the complete set.

# Custard Glass by
# Tarentum Glass Company

Tarentum, Pa.

271-A
**HEART WITH THUMBPRINT**
(oil lamp)

| 272 | 273 | 274 | 275 | 276 | 275 |
|---|---|---|---|---|---|
| **CRUET** (green opaque) | **CRUET** (decorated) | **CRUET** (o.s.) | **TUMBLER** | **PITCHER** | **TUMBLER** |

| 277 | 278 | 279 | 280 | 281 |
|---|---|---|---|---|
| **SPOONER** | **TOOTHPICK** | **BUTTER** | **SUGAR** | **CREAMER** |

*Georgia Gem* (P)

| 282 | 283 | 284 | 285 | 286 | 287 |
|---|---|---|---|---|---|
| **BREAKFAST SUGAR** | **BREAKFAST CREAMER** | **SALT** | **PEPPER** | **MASTER BERRY** | **SAUCE** |

**GEORGIA GEM**—Made by Tarentum, beginning in 1900, this simply designed pattern is growing in popularity. Kamm named it "Little Gem" referring to the small breakfast size creamer, but since the original manufacturer's name for this was "Georgia", Dr. Peterson dubbed the pattern "Georgia Gem". This new name was adopted by the American Custard Glass Association in 1973. Except for the powder jar, all pieces known made are shown in this book (see also Figs. 396 & 399). The pattern is found with or without gilding, and is rare with enamel decorated flowers. **Georgia Gem** was also made in emerald green, plain crystal and in pea green opaque (often called green custard). The feet on this pattern are delicate and highly susceptible to flaking, so take care when purchasing. The cruet, tumbler and salt shakers have no feet, and are sometimes difficult to recognize on sighting. The powder jar and hair receiver are rare without souveniring, so beware of "fixed" pieces.

# Tarentum's Victoria (OMN)

# Heart with Thumbprint

| 288 PITCHER | 289 TUMBLER | 290 CELERY VASE | 291 FINGER LAMP | 292 WINE | 293 KEROSENE LAMP (large size) |

| 294 SUGAR | 295 SPOONER | 296 BUTTER | 297 CREAMER |

| 298 SALT | 299 SAUCE | 300 MASTER BERRY | 299 SAUCE |

**HEART WITH THUMBPRINT** — Pattern glass enthusiasts will claim that the two lamps shown here are not this pattern because the thumbprints are not inside the heart as on the wine and all other pieces to this set. This is ridiculous! Just because the **Alaska** and **Georgia Gem** tumblers do not have feet does not mean they don't belong to their respective sets. Patterns were designed to accomodate the individual pieces. I have seen these lamps named "Trinity" and "Canadian Heart", both of which should once and for all be eliminated!

Note the distinctive enamel decoration, almost identical in style to that found on other Tarentum patterns shown in this book. These lamps are also found in pea green opaque and in emerald green, which should eliminate all doubts as to their origins. They date from 1900. The kerosene lamp came in three different sizes, of which I unfortunately have no dimensions. The largest size is shown here.

Although it appears to be larger (the camera was closer to the subject), Figure 437 is the medium size. The small size is rare.

**TARENTUM'S VICTORIA** — The name of the company should always precede this pattern's name to avoid confusing it for identically named patterns by Riverside, Fostoria and Pioneer Glass Companies. Tarentum's **Victoria** was made only in custard and pea green opaque. All pieces known made are shown here, except for a bud vase. A toothpick holder and cruet were never made. Custard pieces are usually floral decorated with one of an assortment of blossom sprays, but this pattern also came with simple gilding, and with no decoration at all. The pea green color is quite scarce and is seldom found with decoration. Dating from 1900, it apparently had limited production.

# Cane Insert (K)

| 301 SAUCE | 302 MASTER BERRY | 303 SUGAR | 304 SPOONER | 305 PITCHER (green opaque) |

## Tarentum's Tiny Thumbprint (A)

| 306 SPOONER | 307 BUTTER | 308 SUGAR | 309 CREAMER | 310 TOOTHPICK | 311 SALT | 312 PEPPER |

## Panelled Teardrop (P)

| 313 SOUVENIR BUD VASE | 314 SOUV VASE (transfer decor.) | 315 SOUVENIR PITCHER | 316 SOUVENIR WINE | 317 CUSTARD | 318 SUGAR SHAKER |

**CANE INSERT**—For far too long a time this pattern has been called "Button Arches", "Button & Arches", "Button with Arches" and all other imaginable combinations of the two words. This name (or names) has already been assigned to a popular and frequently seen pattern, made in crystal and ruby-stained glass. The two patterns are not the same at all. In Kamm Book 6, plate 51, she shows a covered sugar in the above pattern, naming it **Cane Insert**. This name should once and for all be accepted by collectors. **Cane Insert** was made in custard, pea green opaque and emerald green, sometimes with gold and sometimes without gold. It isn't a very popular pattern, but it is quite scarce, and deserves much more recognition, as it is one of the only custard patterns in an imitation cut design. Introduced in 1899, it was also made a year or so thereafter.

**TINY THUMBPRINT, TARENTUMS** — It is rare that I take the liberty of changing a name, but I strongly feel the need for revising

this one. Kamm named the pattern "Tarentum's Thumbprint" in her Book 5, but her drawing is far from an accurate rendition of the pattern. If it weren't for the fact that there were other "thumbprint" designed patterns which are frequently confused with this one (i.e., **Punty Band**), I would have left well enough alone. The one distinction this pattern has is that the thumbprints are so tiny they are almost entirely indistinguishable when sighting the glass. Thus, the slight addition of the word **tiny** to this pattern's nomenclature, gives it a uniqueness it deserves. The water set and berry set must be extremely rare in custard, as I have never seen them. A very rare cruet was also made. **Tiny Thumbprint** was also made in crystal, green opaque and in ruby-stained glass, and dates from 1904.

**PANELLED TEARDROP**—also made in a salt shaker (Fig. 432); found also in Pea Green opaque.

# Custard Glass by
# *Jefferson Glass Company*

Follansbee, W. Va.

**318-A**
**DIAMOND WITH PEG**
(rare napkin ring)

**318-B**
salt

**318-C**
pepper

**318-D**
toothpick

# Ribbed Drape (G)

| 319 SALT | 320 CRUET (o.s.) | 321 PEPPER | 322 PITCHER | 323 TUMBLER | 324 JELLY |

| 325 SPOONER | 326 BUTTER | 327 CREAMER | 328 SUGAR | 329 TOOTHPICK |

# Jefferson Optic (A)

| 330 SUGAR | 331 BUTTER | 332 SPOONER | 333 MASTER BERRY | 334 SAUCE | 335 TUMBLER |

**RIBBED DRAPE**—Apparently this pattern was officially named (in a book) by Gaddis. It was originally called simply "Jefferson #250" by Kamm and others, but I always prefer names over numbers. It helps collectors grow closer to their glass when they have a name by which to call it. Except for the berry set, all pieces known made are shown here. **Ribbed Drape** is usually found decorated, but undecorated pieces have been seen. The pattern is quite hard to piece together, as most items are scarce. See the color ad reprints on pages 61 & 62.

**JEFFERSON OPTIC**—This pattern has been called simply "Rose" by custard collectors, due to the lovely floral decoration. I named the toothpick to this pattern "Tiny Optic" in Book 1 of my series, not realizing that the toothpick was just part of a larger complete set. With that name totally inadequate now, I toyed with the idea of calling the pattern "Optic Rose" as a compromise, until I found the Figure #403 cruet in this pattern, which was not decorated with roses. Thus, I have settled on the name **Jefferson Optic**, even though a very few pieces to this set lack the optic effect in the glass (seen when held up to a strong light). The water set is very rare—the pitcher is illustrated in Brahmer's book. A creamer and souvenired finger bowl have also been seen in this line. See sectional divider, page 47 for toothpick, and salt & pepper in two decoration variations. The pattern dates quite late, circa 1912. The toothpick has been seen signed "Krys-Tol", a trademark which Jefferson started using about this time.

# Diamond with Peg (P)

| 336 TUMBLER | 337 PITCHER | 338 PITCHER | 339 PITCHER | 340 BUTTER |

| 341 MASTER BERRY | 342 SAUCE | 343 SALT | 344 PEPPER | 345 TOOTHPICK | 346 SHOT GLASS (souv.) | 347 CUSTARD (souv.) |

# Ribbed Thumbprint (k)

| 348 TUMBLER | 349 SOUVENIR CREAMER | 350 INDIVIDUAL OPEN SUGAR | 351 INDIVIDUAL CREAMER | 352 TOOTHPICK | 353 MUG |

**DIAMOND WITH PEG**—In custard glass this was made exclusively by Jefferson, although the pattern was originally made by McKee before 1900. A wide variety of items were produced. Pitchers in six different sizes can be found, from the tiny 2¼" souvenir all the way up to the tankard water pitcher shown here. Occasionally pieces are found signed "Krys-tol", but these are generally souvenir items. In fact, this pattern is found predominately in souvenir items. Non-souvenir "Diamond with Peg" is hard to find, so beware of "fixed" pieces. The napkin ring shown on page 47 is very rare. Also found in crystal and in ruby-stained glass, this pattern is often called "Diamond Peg" for short, which is another accepted name.

**RIBBED THUMBPRINT**—This was Jefferson's #221 pattern, originally introduced about 1907 in crystal only. Later the molds were revived for a run as souvenir ware in custard and ruby-stained glass. No table or water or berry sets have been reported in these colors to date, so if they do exist, they are very rare. All known souvenir items in this pattern are shown here. These custard pieces date around 1912, and are occasionally found signed "Krys-tol".

# Cherry & Scale
## (G)

| 354 | 355 | 356 | 355 |
|---|---|---|---|
| **BUTTER** | **TUMBLER** | **PITCHER** | **TUMBLER** |

| 357 | 358 | 359 | 360 |
|---|---|---|---|
| **SPOONER** | **SUGAR** | **MASTER BERRY** | **SAUCE** |

| 361 | 362 | 363 | 364 |
|---|---|---|---|
| **HORSE MEDALLIONS** | **STALKING LION** | **DRAGON & LOTUS** | **PERSIAN MEDALLION** |

**CHERRY & SCALE**—Apparently the pattern received this name from Gaddis, although it is known as "Fentonia" or "Fentonia Fruit" by carnival glass collectors. It was made only in the water set, table set and berry set, with no other known pieces in the pattern. Made by the Fenton Art Glass Company about 1908, most pieces are usually stained with a nutmeg brown, not unlike that used by Northwood. The pattern is quite hard to piece together. It is very sad that Fenton did not make more of a contribution to the custard glass field, as their custard is rich in color and tone.

**FENTON CUSTARD NOVELTIES**—Figures 361 through 364 are the novelties most often found, although there are undoubtedly others. Both **Horse Medallions** and **Stalking Lion** have been reported in flattened plates (made from the same mold), and these would be scarce. Usually crimped in assorted shapes, Figure 363 is the one most often seen in **Dragon & Lotus.** Note the distinctive fired-on color staining which is so typical of Fenton custard.

# Vermont
(OMN)

365 VASE

366 PICKLE TRAY

367 TUMBLER

368 PITCHER

369 WASTE BOWL

370 SPOONER

371 BUTTER

372 SUGAR

373 CREAMER

374 TOOTHPICK

375 SALT

376 SMALL CARD TRAY

377 MEDIUM CARD TRAY

378 LARGE CARD TRAY

379 SAUCE

380 MASTER BERRY

**VERMONT**—Introduced in 1899 by the U.S. Glass Company, this ivory colored glass was their first attempt to compete in the new market for "custard"-colored glass. Obviously they did not quite get the color right, as this glass is sometimes ignored by "true" custard glass collectors. However, it most decidedly is not milk glass, and is **was** called "ivory" in the original advertisements (see page 66), which is what Northwood called his version. Every shape known is included here in this book, although there is a candle holder (Fig. 408) designed and decorated similarly, which I have name "Jewelled Vermont". **Vermont** is also known as "Honeycomb with Flower Rim", with some sources pointing out that the difference between the two is that one has the honeycombs, while the other does not. The pieces shown here have the honeycomb inside, but since I have never seen a piece without it, and since the ad for **Vermont** specifically said it was made in ivory, I am going to stick to my conclusions presented in Book 1 of this series. I've been told (but it has not been proven to me) that shards of this pattern have been turned up at Greentown's Indiana factory dump. I am hesitant to mention this rumor here, but I suppose it is better to just tell my readers that it is highly unlikely that this pattern was ever made there. U.S. Glass had a factory at nearby Gas City, Indiana, and it is possible that they used the same dump. A celery vase in **Vermont** is shown on page 56. Decoration on the pattern can be blue or green, although undecorated pieces are known.

51

# Custard Souvenirs

| 381 WIDE BAND BELL | 382 WIDE BAND BELL | 383 SOUVENIR PLATE | 384 ROWS OF RINGS VASE | 385 PANEL BOTTOM VASE |

| 386 SOUV. SHOT GLASS | 387 RING & BEADS (souv. creamer) | 388 RING & BEADS | 389 WHIMSEY MUG | 390 WHIMSEY POT | 391 WHIMSEY ALE | 392 6-SIDED NAPKIN RING |

| 393 McKEE HONEYCOMB (wine) | 394 DIAMOND WITH PEG (wine) | 395 JEFFERSON FLEUR-DE-LIS (hair receiver) | 396 GEORGIA GEM (hair receiver) | 397 WASHINGTON | 398 SOUV. CUSTARD CUP |

**CUSTARD SOUVENIRS**—Space permits only a few comments on the pieces shown above which are only a sampling of scores of different souvenir items which were sold at tourist attractions, gift shops, and fairs or were given away as premiums by merchants. Rarely a piece of "advertising custard" can be found, and these pieces would make an impressive collection. It should be noted that most of the souveniring found on these pieces was done by independent firms, not the glass makers.

FIG. 381-382—This bell was probably made by Jefferson, circa 1910. It was made both with and without souveniring, in custard and ruby-stained glass. Note the distinctive rose decoration typical of their products.

FIG. 385—This vase was also made in white opal, which leads me to believe it was made by Heisey, strictly as a souvenir item for an inde-

pendent firm. That is why it probably does not appear in any of their catalogues.

FIG. 387-388—These were made by Jefferson Glass circa 1915. See also Figures 426-427.

FIG. 392—Gaddis incorrectly includes this napkin ring with the **Diamond with Peg** pattern, perhaps due to the identical rose decoration. I understand that this rose decoration was done by an independent decorator firm, Oriental Glass Co.

FIG. 395—This hair receiver and a matching "puff box" were made to imitate the popular **Winged Scroll** pattern, by Jefferson Glass Co., circa 1915. They are usually found souvenired, so beware of suspicious looking scratches on the glass. They are quite scarce without souveniring.

FIG. 397—This is a sugar without a lid. Only the toothpick holder in Washington has been seen without souveniring.

# Miscellaneous Custard Glass

**(Including lamps, "late" custard & miscellaneous additions)**

398-A
(Hanging Lamp)

398-B
(candlesticks)

398-C
(table lamp)

398-D
**McKEE'S FLOWER BAND**

398-E
**McKEE'S FLOWER BAND**

| 399 GEORGIA GEM (celery) | 400 HARVARD (wine) | 401 RIBBED THUMBPRINT (wine) | 402 SOUV. SALT (tall) | 403 JEFFERSON OPTIC (cruet) | 404 PANEL BOTTOM VASE (no souv.) |

| 405 WINGED SCROLL (ash tray) | 406 salt / 407 pepper LEAF COVERED BASE | 408 JEWELLED VERMONT (candlestick) | 409 SAUCE |

*Delaware*
**(Figures 409-414)**

| 410 TUMBLER | 411 BREAKFAST SUGAR (open) | 412 BREAKFAST CREAMER | 413 PIN TRAY | 414 RING TRAY |

LATE ADDITIONS #1—The items pictured on the next seven pages were gathered and photographed during the seven months of production on this book.

FIG. 400 (HARVARD)—The toothpick and the wine are the two items known in custard glass in this pattern, practically always souvenired.

FIG. 403 (JEFFERSON OPTIC)—This cruet is identical to the one shown in Book 3, Fig. 468. The stopper is probably not original. I have only seen two of these cruets, made in an "ivory" colored custard, and both were decorated as above.

FIG. 408 (JEWELLED VERMONT)—This candle holder may or may not belong to the "Vermont" pattern, but it most decidedly

was made by the same company. Millard called this "Palm & Bulls Eye".

FIG. 409-414 (DELAWARE)—No table set, water set or berry set (complete) have been documented to date in this pattern, introduced in 1899 by the U.S. Glass Company. The pattern was produced primarily in emerald green, rose-flashing, crystal and in color-stained crystal. The "ivory" pieces were limited to those shown above, as well as the large creamer and the small round sauce. Any other piece would be most decidedly a rarity.

*Fan*

415
**TRUMPET VASE**

416
**INDIVIDUAL ICE CREAM**

417
**MASTER ICE CREAM**

418
**PLATE**
(Cambridge)

419
**CREASED BALE**
(syrup)

420
**SMOCKING**
(bell)

421
**SERENADE MUG**

422
**PANELLED CANE**
(souv. pitcher)

423
**DAISY BAND**
(shade)

424
**FLORA SCROLL**
(puff box)

425
**SPIDER WEB**
(Alba variant)

426
**RING & BEADS**
(souv. toothpick)

427
**RING & BEADS**
(decor. t.p.)

428
429
**SUNSET**
(salt & pepper)

430
**LITTLE COLUMNS**
(salt)

431
**TINY THUMB-PRINT**
(toothpick)

432
**PANELLED TEARDROP**
(salt)

433
**HARVARD**

LATE ADDITIONS #2

FIG. 416 **(FAN)**—All Ice Cream sets in all patterns were formed from the same molds used on the berry sets. The Fan set shown here is quite rare.

FIG. 419 **(CREASED BALE)**—Made by Dithridge circa 1894-1900. See notes on this pattern in Book 3 of this series.

FIG. 420 **(SMOCKING BELL)**—There is some confusion as to this bell's age, but the custard color is quite authentic. The bell is being reproduced today in all colors imaginable, but I have not seen **any** in custard.

FIG. 421 **(SERENADE MUG)**—This is Indiana Tumbler & Goblet Co.'s single known example of custard glass made at Greentown.

FIG. 427 **(RING & BEADS)**—The toothpick shown with the straight sides is not a souvenir item and is very rare. The pattern was

also made in a tiny creamer, a mug and a vase. Made by Jefferson Glass, circa 1910. Very rare in a water set.

FIG. 428-429 **(SUNSET)**—See notes Book 3 concerning this pattern.

FIG. 430 **(LITTLE COLUMNS)**—Not previously listed, the name was provided by this author. Maker is unknown at this time. Other items in this pattern have not been seen to date.

FIG. 431 **(TINY THUMBPRINT)**—This is a rather choice souvenir toothpick, as it is souvenired "Tulsa, I.T.", the initials meaning "Indian Territory". These, plus those souvenir items with "O.T." (Oklahoma Territory), are quite collectable in that state. They date circa 1902.

FIG. 433 **(HARVARD)**—I can't find a trace of souveniring on this toothpick, making it quite unique, as every other one seen was, or had been, marked with some form of name or date.

| 434 | 435 | 436 | 437 |
|---|---|---|---|
| **SILVER OVERLAY** (Cambridge) | **TROUBADOUR** (goblet) | **VERMONT** (celery vase) | **HEART WITH THUMBPRINT** (med. lamp) |

| 438 | 439 | 440 | 441 |
|---|---|---|---|
| **BEADED CIRCLE** (jelly) | **BEADED SWAG** (pickle) | **BEADED CIRCLE** (tumbler) | **SINGING BIRDS** (mug) |

| 442 | 443 | 444 | 445 | 446 | 447 |
|---|---|---|---|---|---|
| **RARE POLITICAL** commemorative | **HEART** (salt) | **GENEVA** (rust decor.) | **HEART WITH THUMBPRINT** (open sugar) | **LIBBEY'S MAIZE** (ivory t.p.) | **TINY SAWTOOTH** (mini. lamp base) |

LATE ADDITIONS #3

FIG. 435 **(TROUBADOUR)** — This goblet is usually found with souvenir decoration on the bowl of the goblet. However, the above was never stencilled in any manner. I named the pattern Troubadour because of it's classic early English look.

FIG. 439 **(BEADED SWAG)** — This extremely rare little tray is the only other piece of this pattern known in custard, other than the previously illustrated goblet and wine.

FIG. 442 **(POLITICAL COMMEMORATIVE)** — Political or advertising pieces of souvenir custard would make an exciting collection if it weren't for the fact that so few of these were made.

FIG. 444 **(GENEVA)** — This unusual rust-colored decoration is very hard to collect in sets.

FIG. 445 **(HEART WITH THUMBPRINT)** — The tiny breakfast sugar is shown here, which was made to accompany an equally small breakfast creamer.

FIG. 446 **(LIBBEY'S MAIZE)** — This toothpick is in the color often referred to as "custard" color. The husks are decorated in blue, green or red-brown.

| 448 | 449 | 450 | 451 | 452 |
|---|---|---|---|---|
| **NORTHWOOD BLACKBERRY** | **MELON RIB** (mini. lamp base) | **CROCODILE TEARS** (mini. lamp) | **NINE-PANEL** (mini. lamp base) | **PEACOCK AT THE FOUNTAIN** (tumbler) |

| 453 | 454 | 455 | 456 | 457 |
|---|---|---|---|---|
| **NORTHWOOD GRAPE** (puff jar) | **SAILBOAT & WINDMILL** | **LOUIS XV** (blue decor) | **LOW SCROLL** (pin tray) | **LOW SCROLL** (ring tree) |

| 458 | 459 | 460 |
|---|---|---|
| **BLUEBIRDS** | **GRAPE FRIEZE** | **PRAYER RUG** |

## LATE ADDITIONS #4

FIG. 450 (**CROCODILE TEARS**)—I am told by an Indiana, Pa. resident that a lamp just like this in amethyst color was brought home from the local glass factory. I believe it dates around 1905, and Dugan is the likely maker. It was also made in blue and apple green.

FIG. 452 (**PEACOCK AT THE FOUNTAIN**)—I have strong personal doubts as to the age of this tumbler, but only a few have been documented, so they must be rare experimental pieces made by Northwood around 1912, when this pattern was patented.

FIG. 453 (**NORTHWOOD GRAPE**)—Lid is missing on this rare custard puff jar.

FIG. 454 (**SAILBOAT & WINDMILL**)—Made by Fenton around 1908, this tiny sherbert was also formed into a wine glass. The pattern was also used on novelty bowls and on a larger ruffle-edge compote (see Fig. 493).

FIG. 455 (**LOUIS XV**)—I have seen the water set and berry set in this rather garish decorated version on this pattern. Apparently it did not sell well when introduced, as it isn't often found today.

FIGS. 456-457 (**LOW SCROLL**)—These were reportedly made by Fenton around 1910. Fig. 457 is often confused for the Winged Scroll pin tray (see page 37).

Fig. 458 (**BLUEBIRDS**)—Usually found undecorated or with some weak unfired painting on it. Must be Northwood, although I cannot be certain.

FIG. 459 (**GRAPE FRIEZE**)—Definitely Northwood, circa 1908, made in custard, emerald green or cobalt blue—usually found trademarked.

FIG. 460 (**PRAYER RUG**)—Made by Imperial Glass, circa 1910, in custard & carnival colors. Sometimes goofus decorated.

461
**FOOTED WREATH**
(bowl)

462
**SUNSET**
(lamp base)

463
**CHRYSANTHEMUM
TRAY**
(B)

464
**SUNFLOWER
SCROLL**
(nappy)

465  466
**TORCH &
WREATH**
(salt/pepper)

467
**BULGING
TEARDROP**
(condiment set)

468
**WOVEN
CANE**
(salt)

469
**DITHRIDGE
PRINCESS SWIRL**
(condiment set)

470
**HEART**
(t.p.)

471
**CREASED
BALE**
(condiment set)

442  473
**CORN**
(salt/pepper)

*Trailing Vine*

474    475
**MASTER BERRY
&
SAUCE**

476
**COVERED
BUTTER**

477
**SPOONER**

478
**CREAMER**

**LATE ADDITIONS #5**

**FIG. 461 (FOOTED WREATH)**—Named by myself, maker is unknown on this unusual pattern.

**FIG. 463 (CHRYSANTHEMUM TRAY)**—Made in custard and chocolate glass by the Fenton Art Glass Co., this tray was made in two sizes. The larger tray is shown here. The color of custard varies from a rich yellow to a pale "ivory". Name by **Herrick**.

**FIG. 464 (SUNFLOWER SCROLL)**—Made by McKee, circa 1920. Name by **Author**.

**FIG. 465-466 (TORCH & WREATH)**—Made by Dithridge, circa 1899.

**FIGS. 467, 469, 470, 471, 472-473**—All of these were made by Dithridge from 1894 to as late as 1904, when the company merged into the Pittsburgh Lamp, Brass & Glass Co. The condiment holder on the Bulging Teardrop set is original.

**FIG. 468 (WOVEN CANE)**—Made by Coudersport Ornamental Tile & Glass Co., Coudersport, Pa., circa 1901. Found in a condiment set or as individual salt & pepper. Reproduced in cased colors in Japan.

**FIGS. 474-478 (TRAILING VINE)**—Also known as "Endless Vine", this pattern is known only in the table set and berry set. No water set has been documented to date. The covered sugar would be very rare if it exists. I personally have never seen one. Also made by Coudersport Glass, novelties in the pattern were produced in opalescent colors. Name by **Gaddis**.

479
**(candlestick)**

480
**RAM'S HEAD**
**(bowl)**

481

482
**(COMPOTE)**

483
**McKEE'S**
**HONEYCOMB**

484
**FIGURAL FLOWER**
**HOLDER**

485
**SHAVING**
**VESSEL**

486
**ALE GLASS**

487
**DONUT STAND**

488
**ROLLING PIN**

**LATE CUSTARD GLASS** (Circa 1920-1935)

As a "specialist" in the study of Victorian glass, it is rather awkward for me to admit that I know very little about glass made after 1910. I am just getting interested in carnival glass, and maybe ten years from now I will be able to recognize a few depression glass patterns on sight. Thus, I am sorely lacking in knowledge of the glass shown above. Figures 479-482, 484 and 487 were made by the Cambridge Glass Company, of Cambridge, Ohio. McKee and other companies were also involved in production of "late" custard which was very "Art Deco" in style. The examples above are shown only so that readers of this series can familiarize themselves with custard glass made after the decline of the Victorian era.

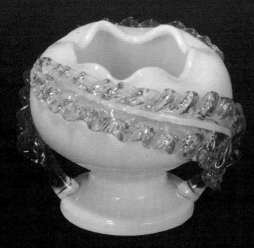

**489**
**ENGLISH VASE**
(applied rigaree)

**490**
**ELK DECORATED ALE**

**491**
**MT. WASHINGTON**
(cracker jar)

**492**
**SUNSET**
(syrup)

**493**
**SAILBOAT & WINDMILL**
(decor. compote)

**494**
**DOUBLE FAN BAND**
(syrup)

**495**
**FANTASIA**
(salt)

**496**
**RIB TWIST**
(salt)

**497**
**SAWTOOTH**
(salt)

**498**
**PANELLED 4-DOT**
(salt)

# Ad & Catalogue Reprints

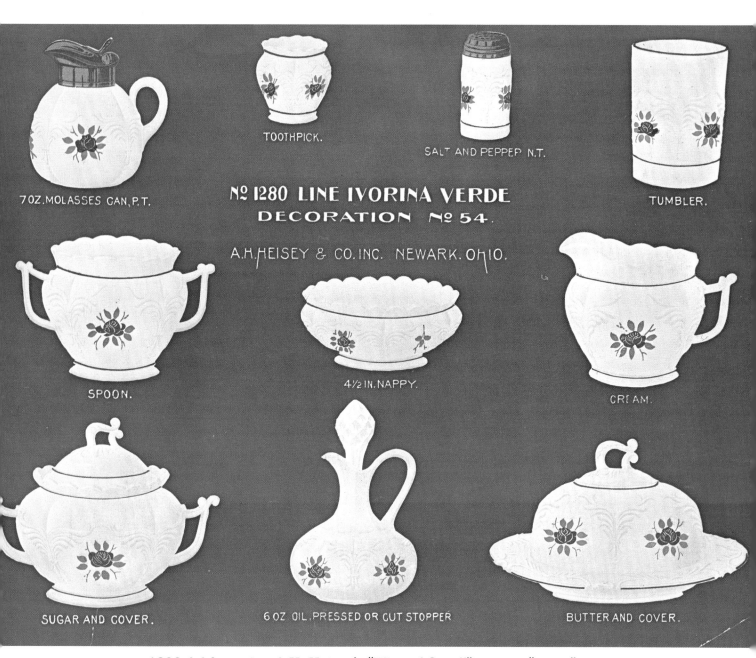

7 OZ. MOLASSES CAN, P.T.

TOOTHPICK.

SALT AND PEPPER N.T.

TUMBLER.

No 1280 LINE IVORINA VERDE
DECORATION No 54.

A.H. HEISEY & CO. INC. NEWARK. OHIO.

SPOON.

4½ IN. NAPPY.

CREAM.

SUGAR AND COVER.

6 OZ OIL. PRESSED OR CUT STOPPER

BUTTER AND COVER.

**1899 Ad featuring A.H. Heisey's "Winged Scroll" pattern "n.o.s."**

## No. 250 Line—Ivory Decorated

**Reprint from original Jefferson Glass Co. catalogue, circa 1904**

**Note the colors made; Kamm incorrectly listed the "blue" as "blue opaque". It is actually a lovely sapphire blue.**

Be sure to see our new Fall Line

# LOUIS XV.
Tableware in Ivory and Gold

## The Northwood Co., Indiana, Pa.

NEW YORK
Frank M. Miller
76 Park Place

PHILADELPHIA
Fitzpatrick & Pascoe
930 Arch Street

BALTIMORE
J. Beiswanger, Jr., & Co.
Moore Building

EAST, George Mortimer          WEST, Carl Northwood

**Special advertisement by The Northwood Co. announcing their new "Louis XV" pattern.**

NORTHWOOD CO.'S NEW LOUIS XV. PATTERN.   IVORY AND GOLD.

**September, 1898 display ad featuring Louis XV.**

FROM THE NEW PHOTOGRAPHIC ASSORTMENT OF W. E. CUMMINGS & CO., CHICAGO, ILL.

**1904 advertisement featuring souvenir glass made by Jefferson, Heisey & Tarentum Glass Companies. These pieces were not souvenired at the factories.**

**1902 advertisement by W. E. Cummings & Co., a manufacturer's jobber. Note the "Ring Band" toothpick featured.**

64

**April, 1903 advertisement by H. Northwood & Co. featuring their "Carnelian" ware, better known today as "Everglades".**

*TEA SET from No. 221 LINE—Three Colors Decorated in Gold and Enamel*

*THE JEFFERSON GLASS CO.*
STEUBENVILLE, OHIO

NEW YORK REPRESENTATIVES
COX & LAFFERTY, 32 Park Place
BALTIMORE REPRESENTATIVES
JOHN A. DOBSON & CO., 110 Hopkins Place
BOSTON REPRESENTATIVES
COX & LAFFERTY, 64 Federal Street

**August, 1905 Ad displaying "Ribbed Thumbprint" table set, not yet documented in custard glass. Only souvenir pieces are known in this pattern.**

65

# Vermont Pattern.

## IVORY DECORATED.

TUMBLER

HALF GALLON PITCHER

Made in assorted tints with hand-painted decorations.

Write us for prices and illustrated catalogue in colors.

**July, 1899 ad prominently featuring their "ivory" decorated "Vermont" pattern. The honeycomb effect in the glass is not distinguishable in the above ad.**

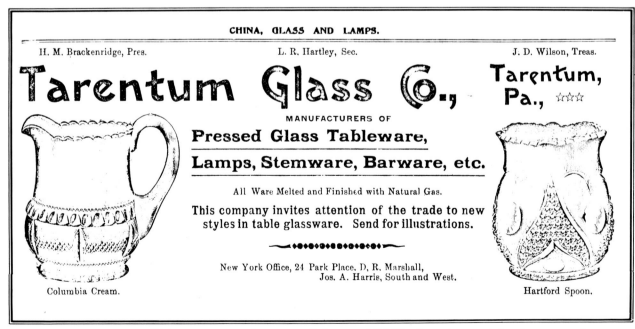

**Advertisement from "China, Glass & Lamps" (circa 1900) showing original names for our "Harvard" & "Heart with Thumbprint" patterns, both of which had limited production in custard glass.**

66

# MORE ADDITIONS AND CORRECTIONS TO BOOK I

| PATTERN | NOTES | PAGE |
|---|---|---|
| QUILTED PHLOX | Shards found at Northwood's Indiana, Pa. site | 37 |
| PANELLED SPRIG | Definitely not Hobbs or Beaumont. This is Northwood-Dugan Glass | 41 |

# MORE ADDITIONS AND CORRECTIONS TO BOOK II

| PATTERN | NOTES | PAGE |
|---|---|---|
| BOGGY BAYOU | This appears to be the same mold used on the vase as is used on the "Reverse Drapery" plate. | 80 |
| DAFFODILS | I have now seen a syrup and a vase in this pattern. Rare in cranberry. NOTE: I am told that the flower on this pattern is not a Daffodil, and I apologize for my blunder. The name appears to be catching on, however, so I will not attempt to change it. | 43 |
| BUTTON PANELS | Since shards of this novelty pattern have been found at the Indiana, Pa. site, we can pretty much assume that the Northwood catalogue which Hartung used so much was put out at this location. | 63 |
| BUBBLE LATTICE | This pattern was apparently made by Hobbs as early as 1890, and later by Northwood-Dugan, circa 1902. Hartung refers to an ad dating this pattern at that time. Shards were found at Indiana, Pa. | 42 |
| POLKA DOT | Old water pitchers now confirmed. Beware of repro's!! | 45 |
| STRIPE, OPALES | Also made in a celery vase and rose bowl. | 46 |
| TWIST, BLOWN | Very rare in cranberry. | 46 |

# ADDITIONS AND CORRECTIONS TO BOOK III

| PATTERN | NOTES | PAGE |
|---|---|---|
| BUBBLE LATTICE | See notes above concerning this pattern. | 17 |
| BLOCKED THUMBPRINT BAND | This pattern was also made in a tankard water pitcher and tumblers. | 16 |
| FLAT DIAMOND BOX | A cruet is now known to exist. | 24 |
| FLAT FLOWER | A sugar shaker was indeed made. | 24 |
| BULBOUS BASE | This pattern can also be found in amber-stained crystal and in frosted "Frances Ware" decoration. | 17 |
| CARMEN | Rare in milk glass. | 18 |
| GRAPE & LEAF | Also made in a water set in decorated milk glass. | 26 |
| GUTTATE | The syrup pitcher and tumbler were reproduced in both shiny and satin finish colors. The tumblers are newly molded and the pattern goes only half-way up the side, whereas the old tumblers have "curtains" all the way up. The syrup is impossible to tell from the originals. | 26 |
| INVERTED THUMBPRINT | Also made in vaseline. Figure 153 (pinched base) was also made in a variant completely lacking the thumbprints. | 28 |
| MAIZE | In all fairness to my opposition, I am told that this pattern *was* made prior to the patent request (at the original New England Glass Co.). However, this is indeed an unusual development. | 32 |
| QUILTED PHLOX | Now known to be Northwood-Dugan at Indiana, Pa. | 37 |
| SAWTOOTHED HONEYCOMB | A toothpick *was* actually made—a charmer, too! | 40 |
| SYNORA LACE | Also made in shiny pidgeon's blood red. | 41 |
| S-REPEAT | Also made in a rare jelly compote. | 41 |
| SWASTIKA | This is probably Northwood-Dugan; I have now seen the water pitcher in unusual tankard shape, and in blue opalescent!! | 43 |